STORIES MAKE THE WORLD

STORIES MAKE THE WORLD

Reflections on Storytelling and the Art of the Documentary

Stephen Most

berghahn
NEW YORK · OXFORD
www.berghahnbooks.com

First published in 2017 by

Berghahn Books

www.berghahnbooks.com

Library of Congress Cataloging-in-Publication Data

Names: Most, Stephen, author.
Title: Stories make the world : reflections on storytelling and the art of the
    documentary / Stephen Most.
Description: New York : Berghahn Books, 2017. | Includes bibliographical
    references and index.
Identifiers: LCCN 2017012306 (print) | LCCN 2017021569 (ebook) | ISBN
    9781785335778 (eBook) | ISBN 9781785335754 (hardback : alk. paper) |
    ISBN 9781785335761 (pbk. : alk. paper)
Subjects: LCSH: Documentary films—History and criticism. | Documentary
    films—Authorship.
Classification: LCC PN1995.9.D6 (ebook) | LCC PN1995.9.D6 M615 2017 (print)
    | DDC 070.1/8—dc23
LC record available at https://lccn.loc.gov/2017012306

British Library Cataloguing in Publication Data

A catalogue record for this book is available from the British Library

ISBN: 978-1-78533-575-4 (hardback)
ISBN: 978-1-78533-576-1 (paperback)
ISBN: 978-1-78533-577-8 (ebook)

For Rachel & Jonah

with love & admiration

CONTENTS

PART FIVE: THE ANTHROPOCENE

 **INTRODUCTION**

We tell ourselves stories in order to live.
—Joan Didion

Fire on Earth, if spotted by creatures living elsewhere in our galaxy, would serve as evidence of life on this planet. Fire needs oxygen. Plant photosynthesis releases oxygen into Earth's atmosphere, and animal respiration cycles this oxygen, keeping the supply in stable balance.

Long before there were human beings, those aliens, having seen fire, could have predicted that intelligent life would arise on Earth with the emergence of a species able to carry, control, and use combustion.

The Promethean spark was ignited about a million years ago when Homo erectus and other hominids walked the Earth.[1] The generation of warmth, enabling bands to migrate into and survive within cold climes; the flames that protected them from predators; the increase in calories that came from burning animal habitats for hunting and scavenging; and the ability to cook food, reducing the energy needed for digestion, were powerful factors in hominid evolution, making possible the growth of a brain able to invent symbolic forms.

According to neuroscientist Antonio Damasio, storytelling emerged at the dawn of "full-fledged human consciousness." Imagining "early humans sometime after verbal language established itself as a means of communication," he concluded that narratives have shaped human identity and cultural evolution ever since.[2] Thanks to fire, and often by firelight, human beings have told the stories that make our worlds.

Stories make the world, for "the world" is not a fixed entity. Although the term refers to natural places and human creations that endure over the ages, these change continually as subjects for discourse and arenas for action. The world connects and separates people who, influenced by stories, maintain and expand the web of human relationships or differ in ways that tear it apart. Some groups assert an identity that defines others out of their world, categorically rejecting them as evil, ungodly, or less than human. Some include all of humanity within their world, others all of life; and people from the beginnings of human life have experienced a world that encompasses all of nature from the stars above to the ground beneath their feet.

We need stories to orient ourselves within the flood of impressions and the multitude of possibilities. Hannah Arendt thought that in order to say what is, to distinguish reality from "the totality of facts and events, which, anyhow, is unascertainable," a person "always tells a story, and in this story the particular facts lose their contingency and acquire some humanly comprehensible meaning."[3] According to Atul Gawande, "Life is meaningful because it is a story, and a story's arc is determined by the moments when something happens."[4]

Stories hold groups together in shared associations over vast reaches of time and space. They inspire transformational events, including wars and revolutions, and make reconciliation with adversaries possible. Personal stories, imagined and remembered, mark the continuity of a life while explaining changes in roles and situations. Stories are so intrinsic to being human that their influence can be taken for granted, just as people may take health for granted until illness affects their lives.

Today, when individuals have more access to international travel, information, and communications than has previously been possible, humanity has a common objective world yet one whose subjective boundaries continue to shift, its lines drawn as much by stories as by armies and alliances. Today, when an unprecedented variety of apparently true accounts is accessible to all, those who seek understanding have to find their bearings. Choices about who speaks truly and what is right can matter greatly not only in guiding individual lives and the course of nations but also humanity's response to the global impacts of Promethean fire.

※

This is a book about nonfiction storytelling. In writing it, I have woven together four strands: reflections on storytelling as a crucial human activity whose forms, from primeval firelight to lighted screens, include ceremonies, theater, paintings, photography, and movies as well as the spoken and written word; profiles of individuals, some of whom I have known, whose storytelling has had an enduring influence; inquiries into the subjects of various documentary films and the choices involved in representing them; and insights based on my experiences as a filmmaker in turning a wide range of subjects into stories for documentaries.

Investigating a subject from multiple points of view is a skill that reporters, playwrights, and documentary makers have in common. Through the process of developing a story worthy of public attention that makes sense from all credible perspectives, one attains an impartial viewpoint. The work that results offers neither *an* opinion nor *the* truth but a way of looking at things based on valid sources.

The combination of cinematography with the recording of ambient sound and spoken words makes documentaries a compelling form of nonfiction storytelling. Documentaries make it possible to see things from unfamiliar vantage points, to go almost anywhere, and, via archival film, to travel through time. Yet their use of actual sounds and images does not ensure truthful depictions of reality. Documentary is necessarily an art of illusion. Its carefully selected and edited content reaches the public after audio mixing, color correction, and other forms of technical manipulation. Nonfiction filmmakers can portray any subject in a variety of ways, with emphasis on different characters, themes, and events, each version yielding a different meaning.

More than accurate representations of sounds and images on the screen, what gives these works credibility are the makers' methods and integrity. Everyone's view of reality is shaped by the particularities of each life. The art of making nonfiction films includes methods for overcoming, or compensating for, those limitations. Rather than impose a meaning or preformulated opinion upon the material, the conscientious artist explores a subject with an open mind, in search of knowledge from numerous vantage points, often spending years on one project. This process contrasts strongly with the rapid production and distribution of content by commercial and social media, many of whose makers send out—and whose consumers seek out—information and opinions that echo their existing views.

The veracity of a nonfiction film matters especially when it presents an alternative to the acceptable range of subjects and interpretations that support the powers-that-be. When a documentary that represents reality independently and impartially challenges the political and nationalistic partiality of news sources and the ideological partiality of believers and propagandists, it must be able to withstand charges of bias and factual error.

Impartiality is not the same as objectivity—a standard mistakenly applied in judging documentaries. Like the storytellers whose lives I portray, and in contrast both to writers of fiction who have no commitment to factuality and to reporters whose stories' primary purpose is to impart information, I choose subjects I find meaningful. Objectivity implies the absence of personal interest. Impartiality results from a journey that, from the beginning, matters to the writer, filmmaker, or other teller of tales, then moves beyond personal interest toward a horizon that interests the public at large.

How then does one begin? The measure of a good beginning, Ian McEwan wrote, "is how much sense it makes of what follows."[5]

For me, the beginning came when I encountered Erik H. Erikson's concept of the "identity crisis," which helped me come to terms with youthful feelings of confusion and alienation. This idea concerns the loss of ability to grasp the continuity of one's self as situations change. However it comes about, an identity crisis can be described as an absence or breakdown of the story that gives meaning to life and guides a person's actions.

Erikson taught a freshman seminar that I took my first year in college. He was an innovative storyteller, interpreting the lives of world leaders in light of his clinical experiences as a psychoanalyst. He even sought to understand the beliefs of a California Indian tribe in relation to their childrearing practices and the ecology of their riverine homeland. After the course was over, Erikson agreed to guide me in an independent major looking at the relationship between societies, their mythologies, and their environments—between their stories, that is, and their worlds.

Erikson's support led to a stroke of fortune: an anthropologist who was one of his colleagues gave me a field studies grant to go to Peru. There I met Pedro Azabache, an artist, and Eduardo Calderón, a shamanic healer. Azabache's paintings of his Moche Indian milieu in conjunction with the journal he kept suggested a form of storytelling that combines visual representation with verbal expression. Calderón's dramatic ceremonies made me think freshly about the roots of theater, for at the time, I had no knowledge of documentary making; my identity revolved around playwriting. Only years later did it occur to me that the magic of seeing across great distances, even across the divide between the living and the dead, which shamans activate, is achieved through the technologies of nonfiction film.

The ability to think across great distances and differences in order to throw light on contemporary events was Hannah Arendt's exceptional skill. Having found in her work a profound yet unconventional understanding of civilization and the catastrophes of the twentieth century, I went to graduate school to study with her. Of value to me also was Arendt's love of theater and her grasp of the ideas underlying the power of tragedy. I did not anticipate that her thoughts about the origins and importance of impartiality would influence my work not only as a playwright but also as a filmmaker.

Arendt spoke about "the inalienable right to go visiting," a right I exercise in traveling and in making friends with strangers. Writers are typically advised to "write what you know," yet I learned from my mentors and from experience that writing is an excellent vehicle for exploring what and whom one does not know.

Throughout my journey, documentary making—usually as a screenwriter, sometimes as a producer—has enlarged my world.[6] I hope that the stories I tell about nonfiction storytelling and about people I have known, whether personally or via projects, will enlarge yours as well.

PART ONE

STORYTELLERS

To be a person is to have a story to tell.
—Isak Dinesen

No philosophy, no analysis, no aphorism, be it ever
so profound, can compare in intensity and richness
of meaning with a properly narrated story.
—Hannah Arendt

▦ PEDRO AZABACHE

In 1964, I traveled to Peru's north coast. I was an undergraduate, and although I had not studied anthropology, a professor gave me a field studies grant to do ethnographic research near the Moche River, which flows from the Andes to the Pacific, watering an otherwise lunar landscape along the way.

At the time I was wondering who I was, how I should live, and what was worth doing. I thought that seeing those questions reflected in the lives of others and in other ways of life could bring me closer to finding out what was personally meaningful.

I had read about Pedro Azabache and wanted to meet him.[1] He lived south of the city of Trujillo on a farm near the town of Moche. The leader of the summer field studies program, a graduate student, had other ideas. He regarded anthropology as a science, and that, for him, meant collecting data that, with the aid of theories and equations, could make a durable contribution to the knowledge of mankind. He spent his summer in a rented room by a truck stop on the Pan-American Highway counting all the buses, trucks, cars, and cycles that passed by. He did not record the art that drivers painted on their vehicles— hearts, flowers, or designs displaying the names of wives and girl-friends. He had no use for subjective facts. He wanted Cartesian data, raw information.

Why, then, study the life of an individual? Pedro Azabache was a Moche Indian, and anthropologists study indigenous people, true enough. But Azabache was no exemplar of a traditional culture. He was an outlier, a unique person. Having graduated from a school of fine arts in Lima, Azabache headed an arts institute in Trujillo. I argued that his life story would open a window onto the culture of Moche and so would his paintings, which portray everyday life in the town and countryside of his native ground. Moreover, as an artist Azabache connected the present day with the ancient past; for the coastal farmlands irrigated by the Moche River are the ancestral home of the Mochica, a pre-Incaic civilization known for artistic brilliance that reached its peak about a thousand years ago. Beyond the irrigated land, two weathered pyramids made of massive adobe bricks rise from the desert: the Temple of the Sun and the Temple of the Moon. Had I been making documentaries at the time, I would have realized that Azabache's narrative and his art, when combined with images of the legacy of his Mochica ancestors, offered a graphic sense of his world that I could share with others.

I caught a collective cab on the Pan-American Highway heading toward Moche. The *colectivo* stopped at the town's plaza near its double-towered church. I got out along with five Mocheros and the pig that one of the women held in a cloth bag close to her chest. I could tell they were Mocheros. Their features and facial expressions resembled people portrayed on the stirrup-spouted ceramic sculptures of Mochica artists. Dug out from desert sands and displayed on museum shelves, Mochica pottery seemed to represent everything the ancients knew and imagined: fantastic creatures with human faces and fangs; birds' heads with human bodies; gods wielding scepters; shapely gourds and tubers; pelicans, jaguars, sea lions, crabs and other wildlife; fellatio and copulation; a women giving birth, the baby crowning; a woman drumming; a man with a skin disease, without a nose; a whistling shaman; a warrior and his captive; and portraits of myriad individuals, their heads topped by the spout of the pot. Many centuries later, the people of Moche were living in a different world from that of their ancestors, but they looked the same.

At the edge of town, I saw the Mochica pyramids and marveled. As I walked along a dirt road between adobe walls and irrigation ditches that bordered sunken fields, a barefoot boy, about twelve years old, wearing blue workpants, a checkered shirt, and a sombrero, approached me. The boy asked, "*¿Qué razón?*" and without waiting for an answer walked on.

The mysterious question reverberated in my mind. "*¿Qué razón?*"— for what reason? Why was I there, on that continent, among strangers? What did this place where people spoke a language I barely knew have to do with my life? Why did I want to learn about a stranger's life?

I climbed the larger of the two adobe pyramids, the Huaca del Sol, and looked toward the Pacific. Its waves, I thought, wash the shores of my California homeland. Geographically, I was on the same planet. But *¿qué razón?*—for what reason the life and death of Mochica civilization, and of the Chimú who conquered them, and the Inca who conquered them, and the Spanish who conquered them? Was there some destiny or underlying logic to this history? Is there a more than physical continuity between the people of Moche and their ancestors? What remained, what was lost, what was disappearing, what was changing into something new? And what did this history have to do with the life of Pedro Azabache or myself or anyone else? Unable to answer these questions, I fell into a reverie.

Hours later, as the reddening Sun seared the horizon, I walked to the Pan-American Highway, caught a *colectivo*, and went to Trujillo. That night, I was sitting in a restaurant waiting for dinner when a man at a nearby table turned to his companion and asked, "*¿Qué horas son?*" (*¿Qué 'ras son?*) What time is it? That, I suddenly realized, is what the boy wanted to know; he expected the *gringo* to have a watch! That question had an answer.

I was looking for meaning. He wanted information. Actually, the question "What time is it?" has answers of both kinds: a fact measured by the position of a shadow, the hands of a clock, the spin of an atom— and meaning, which comes from stories.

☼

"I want to remember my times," wrote Pedro Azabache, beginning a journal when he was an art student in Lima. Remembering helped the young man maintain his sense of identity in spite of the stark disjunction between *la campiña* (the countryside) and the modern city, between the cyclical time of an indigenous farmer and the linear time of an urban individual.

In 1925, when Pedro Azabache was six years old, Mocheros lived in rooms covered with mats of bulrush or without any roofs at all. That March, a catastrophic rainstorm flooded Moche farmland. Its inhabitants panicked. The Azabaches ran through the torrent, terrified by lightning, seeking shelter. Overflowing its banks, the river drowned cows, burros, and horses in waters dark with soil. Invading the coastal desert, flooding defaced the Huaca del Sol, with adobe walls tumbling and ancient murals washed away.

As the century progressed, slower forces eroded the way of life of a people who had lost their language long before the *conquista* yet retained traditional customs until modern times. Roads and cars brought Mocheros to places they had never been before. Education expanded their mental horizons. Tractors replaced plows; trucks as well as burros transported corn, sweet potatoes, and cans of milk; kilns turned farmland into bricks for sale as the population grew and cities spread across the sands.

Pedro Azabache's parents were farmers who wanted their boys to get an education. The year after the flood, they sent him and his brother Gasper to seminary school in Trujillo, a three-mile walk. On the way, the boys prepared their lessons. Back home, they watered the cattle, did other farm work, and helped their father, Don Manuel, build a new house. It was a hard schedule that took a strong will.

At the seminary school, Father Serna painted with oils on canvas, and he encouraged Pedro, who loved to draw, to paint as well. The boy painted Christ's heart, landscapes, and other images he copied from stamps and pictures in magazines. Although the priest taught indoors, he told his students to seek out beauty in nature since nature's beauty is the counterpart of God's beauty. Pedro disliked Serna's philosophy. For him what mattered was immediate experience, not ethereal divinity. In Trujillo, he met a group of artists who taught him techniques for painting landscapes. One day when he went to their house, they had gone, and his art supplies were gone with them.

Don Manuel wanted his son to be a lawyer, but when, after graduating from seminary, Pedro declared that he wanted to paint, his father said, "Fine" and gave him enough money to support himself for three months. In 1937, Pedro moved to Lima, where his sister Rosa was living, to study at the School of Fine Arts.

At this point, the young Mochero entered a current that had risen with the Mexican Revolution. The director of the *Escuela Nacional de Bellas Artes* (National School of Fine Arts), José Sabogal, was a Peruvian of Spanish descent who, when painting in Cuzco, became inspired by pre-Columbian art. Traveling through Mexico in 1922, Sabogal met Orozco, Rivera, and Siqueiros, the revolutionary muralists who portrayed pyramids and factories, Aztecs and industrialists, slaves in a mine and workers on strike in their depictions of history and the modern world. In an era when Peruvian painters were imitating European masters, Sabogal fostered cultural nationalism, *indigenismo*, to honor his land and its native reality. He encouraged Peruvian artists to paint Peruvian themes.

In Sabogal's academy, Azabache learned how to render complicated subjects into simple lines and shapes. When a student's sketch contained too many details and colors, he recalled, Sabogal would have him look at the bold essential form of a Mochica portrait pot.

When his sister died and their family came to Lima to hold a mass in her honor, Azabache made pencil sketches. Sabogal saw a study of the family in the kitchen preparing lunch. He encouraged the Mochero to draw at home; and when Azabache returned from vacation with a stack of sketches, the master granted him freedom from attending classes; he had only to take the exam.

To celebrate his graduation, Don Pedro exhibited his work in a gallery in Lima. "For those who attended," he recalled, "I made a Mochero-style meal of *cebiche* and *chicha* because one of my paintings showed women preparing such a meal. We all got drunk."

Aided by alcohol, Azabache's paintings enlarged the art lovers' world. In Peru, the chasm between indigenous people and members of the dominant society who, like Sabogal, descended from Europeans, ran deep. Indians were at the bottom of a class system that relegated them to brutal labor at abysmal wages and that, in the *haciendas*, put them under the control of feudal lords before whom they bowed abjectly. Their languages, predominantly Quechua, separated them further from non-Indian Peruvians. People like Pedro Azabache who spoke Spanish and who lived on and lived off the lands of their ancestors made up a small fraction of Peru's native population. Unlike the *indigenista* painters who, turning away from European subjects, looked at native Peru from the outside, Azabache learned from European masters as well as from the arts of ancient Moche how to portray it from the inside. Yet bridging these worlds came at a cost to the young Mochero, opening a chasm within himself.

For six months in 1945, Azabache aided Sabogal in the creation of frescoes at the Hotel Cuadro in Cuzco. He almost didn't go there. Shortly before leaving, "there were eruptions over my whole body," Pedro wrote in his notebook. "Afraid I would not be able to go to Cuzco, I visited the *brujo* [medicine man] in Ferrañafe. He cured me in one night. At his *mesa* [an all-night healing session] sat people who were convalescing after other *mesas*. But this *mesa* was dedicated to me. The *brujo* knew many things about me. He asked me, 'What is art?' and I explained a few things. He told me someone had cast a spell over me and described a distant cousin who had lived with me in Lima and stole my clothes. The *brujo* then gave me something very bitter to drink. I remember nothing after that, but the next morning I was completely cured."

Besides Sabogal, Azabache regarded José Eulogio Garrido as a formative influence. Garrido was a writer whose literary circle, *Grupo Norte*, included the poet César Vallejo and the pan-American revolutionary Victor Raúl Haya de la Torre. Garrido edited the Trujillo newspaper, *La Industria*, ran an archaeology museum, and served as the mayor of Moche. He lived alone in Moche, with the aid of servants, in a palatial house. Hanging on its white walls in room after room were paintings by contemporary Peruvian artists.

Garrido was a strong character. To hear him say, in his high-pitched voice, *por su puesto!* (of course!) was to feel certainty in its purest form. Over the years, the writer and the artist went on excursions together. They looked for inspiration in the Andes and explored nearby places including Huanchaco, a coastal town where men fish from reed boats like the fishermen on Mochica pots, and Chan Chan, the high-walled adobe city of the Chimú.

Chan Chan, like the Huaca del Sol, is severely eroded. Don Pedro liked it that way: a labyrinth of powerful ochre forms beneath strips of blue sky. Garrido, for his part, championed the archaeological study and restoration of Chan Chan. His museum hired Eduardo Calderón, a sculptor who made ceramics in the Mochica manner, to re-create the murals on the inner walls of the Chimú city.

More than many other Mocheros, Azabache lived traditionally. When I met him, he was living with his mother, Maria Dolores Bustamante, in the house his father built. He and his brother Gaspar gave her one half of the proceeds from their land, just as they had when Don Manuel was alive. Every day he worked in the fields growing corn and sweet potatoes. Electricity had not yet come to *la campiña*; candles lit the adobe homes. Don Pedro and his mother ate, as was customary, sitting on an earthen floor. Their food was spiced with *aji*, a potent pepper the Mochica grew, often portrayed on sculpted pots. They had no bathroom or outhouse; people fertilized the fields. They sunbaked rectangular molds of clay and straw to build with. In this and many other respects, the Azabaches lived as their ancestors had for centuries.

Yet more than other Mocheros, Don Pedro was a modern man. His friends were artists and intellectuals. Although his house was made of adobe, he had a kiln that produced *ladrillos*, the fired red bricks that modern buildings are made of. And every weekday, he put on a suit and went to Trujillo to teach painting in his school of fine arts.

In those years, several decades before the Huaca de la Luna was restored and tourist buses drove there though the farmlands, many Mocheros thought the pyramids in the desert were made by the Incas, not their own ancestors. But Don Pedro believed that his artistic vision came in a direct line of descent from the Mochica masters. Just as Rivera was versed in Aztec and Mayan art, Azabache rooted his creativity in the traditions of his country. Like Sabogal, he admired Mochica pottery more than the ceramics of ancient Greece, not only for its esthetic value but because those works declare clearly, "This is how we are."

Azabache's paintings witnessed the traditional Mochero way of life at the very time that electrification, education, exposure to mass media, and migration to urban jobs were transforming it irreversibly. He feared the loss of "how we are." Just as his brick factory was turning the soil of Moche into buildings, pressures of modern life were uprooting the soul of Moche.

His art went beyond representing the surface of appearances. One night at a restaurant, Don Pedro picked up a green glass bottle. "This is not *cerveza* [beer]," he said; "this is *belleza* [beauty]." He explained, "There is a great difference between the watchful eye of an artist, whether he be a painter, sculptor, poet, or architect, and the eye of a man who is not an artist. The eye of a man of true feeling is one that discovers in nature great plasticity and spiritual richness for the sake of those who have neither vision nor a feeling for nature. The painter sees in nature images, discovers immense masses of movement and color, in anything, whether it be in trees, in animals, in plants, in clouds in the sky."

Asked what an artist sees in other human beings, the painter responded, "Everyone in the world without exception has a great heart, a heart of distinct feelings. An artist discovers that men who have hearts do not see the richness of their own hearts. That is the difference that an artistic man sees between himself and a man who is not an artist. And the artistic man wishes that every man in the world could have the feeling of an artist because that will be the one fountain from which a common vision and love for nature will flow."

Here was another answer to "*¿Qué razón?*": to experience the richness of the moment, the time it is, on this Temple under the Sun.

○

When he died in 2012 at the age of 94, Pedro Azabache was known as an artist whose life and work bridged the historic, economic, and social divide between indigenous and modern Peru. Helping him cope with the tension of combining traditional life on a farm in Moche with involvement in the urban art world were his journals.

Remembering his days with a pen while portraying his world with a paintbrush gave Don Pedro a sense of continuity. Writing brought to the richness of experience the dimensionality of memory and reflection. Ever since that summer in Moche, for every project I've embarked on, whether a film, a book, or a play, I have kept a journal, recording the information and the adventures, discoveries and disappointments, confusions and realizations along the way.

A basic lesson of nonfiction impressed itself on me while writing about Azabache with the aid of his journals, at the home of the maestro, with access to his family, friends, and students: namely, basic facts can be hard to pin down. When I spoke with various people to confirm an event that a journal entry recorded, I often heard contradictory accounts. In some cases, the elusiveness of memory showed its hand; in others, divergent perspectives from which witnesses viewed the same occurrence.

Nonfiction storytelling parts company from fiction regarding the importance of getting the facts right. A creative writer or screenwriter has the license to make facts up. These can be far more convincing and satisfying than what actually happened. Facts in themselves are arbitrary. The date a person was born, the number of cattle killed in a flood, the location of a battlefield, the name of the victor—these have no inherent meaning. When such facts are part of a nonfictional story, one can expect that they, rather than an entirely different set of facts, will make some kind of sense, but the made-up facts in fictions "ring true."

A different distinction separates the commitment to factuality of the nonfiction storyteller from the scientist's collection of data. For the former, facts are the foundation for a true story. They are a necessary condition for understanding a subject, which is the basis for its meaningful representation. In contrast, for the scientist, facts are information that may contribute to but remains separate from any particular interpretation. Even when a theory successfully accounts for all the facts, scientists look for contradictory information while considering alternative theories that could explain the facts in a different way.

This distinction between raw information and potentially meaningful content has taken on new significance as artificial intelligence both augments and replaces human cognition in such fields as translation, personal identification, and medical diagnosis. "The birth of information theory," observed science historian James Gleick, "came with its ruthless sacrifice of meaning—the very quality that gives information its value and its purpose."[2] The ability of a computer program to apply a set of instructions translating a story in Chinese into English does not enable it to understand the contents of the story—an insight that led philosopher John Searle to make his "Chinese Room" argument. "Searle simply argued," explained science and technology writer John Markoff, "that a computing machine is little more than a very fast symbol shuffler that uses a set of syntactical rules. What it lacks is what the biological mind has—the ability to interpret semantics."[3]

However powerful, omnipresent, useful, and voluminous as information has become in our time, it cannot replace the human need for meaning. For that we rely, as we have from the dawn of human awareness, on storytelling.

EDUARDO CALDERÓN

What is real? Members of a symbol-minded species, we mix dreams with waking awareness, fantasies with perceptions, lies and tall tales with truth telling. Yet to be real in the world, phenomena have to be manifest in some way. Just as photons and planets must be observed to rate as data, thoughts and dreams are unreal if not remembered and conveyed; they have to be *real*ized. Descartes may doubt everything except that he thinks, but unless he says that he thinks and therefore exists, that idea does not exist, for a documentary maker at least.

Even the most passionate thoughts, feelings, and delights "lead an uncertain, shadowy kind of existence," noted Hannah Arendt, "unless and until they are transformed, deprivatized and deindividualized, as it were, into a shape to fit them for public appearance." When "we talk about things that can be experienced only in privacy or intimacy, we bring them out into a sphere where they will assume a kind of reality which, their intensity notwithstanding, they never could have had before."[1]

By bringing private experience into the open, storytelling plays a role in forming friendships and in psychological healing, whether from an analyst's couch or a *brujo's mesa*.

A master of shamanic storytelling was Eduardo Calderón, who taught wood and ceramic sculpture at Pedro Azabache's School of Fine Arts.

One day, when I was watching young artists paint at the Trujillo academy, Calderón asked me to visit him in Las Delicias, a beach town south of Moche. "I'd like to do your portrait in clay," he said.

His house was hard to find. There were no street names, and the adobe buildings looked alike. But I knew I had knocked on the right door when children appeared shouting, *"El gringo! El gringo!"* After greeting me, Calderón introduced me to his wife María, a Mochera. "She's a *huaco*," he said. "The portrait pots look just like her."

The studio was a partly roofless, partly mat-covered room near the adobe-walled courtyard. A large fishing net lay coiled in a corner. On a shelf rested replicas of Mochica *huacos*, complete with stirrup spouts, including one whose model was clearly María, with her broad, pleasant face, her black hair in a braid. A bust of Pedro Azabache looked on as I sat in a chair and the sculptor took his position standing next to a small round table. María brought us a wooden bowl of *chicha*, a thick sweet corn liquor that we took turns drinking.

Our conversation quickly turned to religion. It was mainly a monologue, with Calderón speaking too quickly for me to follow everything he said, but so expressively that I felt I understood. When his eyes narrowed and a quick gesture pulled a narrow beard from his chin, the sculptor was Confucius. When his hands molded in air an extension of his belly, his eyes now fixed in a gaze, he was the Buddha and not just talking about him.

"What is your religion?" he asked me. I said I am a Jew. "Are Jews baptized?" asked Calderón, explaining he had never met a Jew before. As I answered questions about Judaism, the sculptor pulled clay out of a long cylinder and plopped it onto the round table. He made great gobs of clay, rolled them, and slapped them onto the mass. "Do you know," he asked, "that I am a *brujo*?"

Calderón invited me to attend his next *mesa*, at Pedro Azabache's house where I was staying, the following Tuesday night. This would be a healing session. *Curanderos,* or healers like Calderón, are a kind of *brujo,* for they use all-night *mesas* as do their counterparts, the *brujos* who practice sorcery. A healer's *mesa* is the antidote to the sorcerer's bewitchment.

It was dark when Calderón arrived in the *campiña* of Moche. He carried a white sack of objects for the *mesa*. His assistant, a wizened man wearing a seaman's cap, carried a bundle of swords and staffs. As the site for the *mesa*, Calderón chose a place between the maestro's house and a row of trees.

The other participants were waiting for him: Don Pedro, his brother Gaspar, a nephew named Fernando, several other Mocheros who had come to assist their neighbor and to be cured of their own ailments, José Li Ning, a medical student who studied art with Azabache, *Doctora* Lucile Loeser, a psychiatrist who also studied at the *Escuela,* and myself. Ironically, by refusing to do what my group leader considered anthropology, I had landed in an ethnological paradise.

We stood around as Calderón sprinkled the site with holy water and laid three cloths down, white muslin on top. Facing east, away from the house, the *brujo* stuck the swords and staffs in the ground along one edge of the *mesa*. Crouching, he placed objects, each with a kiss, upon the *mesa*, then lined several small bottles up beside him. After rising and surveying the layout, he wound a white cloth around his head.

In the darkness, with the slender moon hidden behind trees and the white muslin covered by objects, the healer's turban was brighter than anything else. For those who sat to his left and right sides along the *mesa* and for the patients who stood on the open space across from the *brujo*, his head was the focus of attention.

Calderón asked, "*¿Qué horas son?*" It was after nine. He lifted one of the bottles and spewed perfume water over the *mesa*. He began to pray in Latin, Quechua, and Spanish, alternating prayers with long drinks from a can containing a thick liquid. This was a boiled-down mix of water and slices from the San Pedro cactus, which, like peyote, is a natural source of mescaline.

The *brujo* picked up a rattle and, accompanying himself, sang a song encompassing the entire world. Lyrically, it complemented the *mesa*, a symbolic microcosm at his feet.

> I come entering
> with my singing
> with my powers
> with my herbs and
> with my sugar candy
> all the mountains
> all the seven mountains
> seven fortunes
> seven churches
> of the whole world.
> Up the sierra
> down the coast and
> in the mighty jungle
> I come entering
> where I'm singing
> I come entering
> where I'm playing
> playing, playing.
> Help me San Cipriano
> light my path and
> take me far with
> all my powers
> with my herbs and
> with my sugar candy.

After singing for a long while, telling the story of his shamanic journey across "the whole world," Calderón passed the can around. The liquid was intensely bitter; I had a hard time getting it down. Calderón said that we would be seeing things. Holding a dagger in his left hand, he assured us we were safe, protected by the *mesa*. But he warned us to keep watch on the sky. Since it was Tuesday, other *brujos* would be practicing, and if a light appeared in the sky, it could mean some evil *brujo* had spotted this *mesa* and might attack.

A Mochera stood before the *mesa* across from the *brujo*. Calderón's assistant, known as the *alzador*, or lifter, stood next to her. Through each nostril, he drank from an oyster shell a mixture of lemon, tobacco juice, San Pedro, and *pisco*, a grape liquor. The *alzador* refilled the pointed shell, pouring the concoction from a small can, and gave it to the woman. She lifted the shell slowly to her nose, tilted her head back, let the potion enter her nostrils, and suddenly bent over, belching convulsively. Then she returned to her standing position facing Calderón. He stared at the line of swords and staffs. "Did you see one vibrate?" he asked the *alzador*, who said he did not. After a long silence, Calderón told the Mochera to pull up a staff on which the figure of a saint was carved. She took it, stepped back from the *mesa*, and stood rigidly at attention.

The *brujo* said he saw someone standing beside her. "Someone in your family. Someone in your family is troubling you." The woman nodded. "One of your children. Yes, I see it is a girl. Your daughter?" The woman said that her daughter had run away a week before. "Don't worry, I will find her. Did you bring me some of her clothing?" The Mochera handed him a piece of cloth, which Calderón placed upon the *mesa*. He whistled awhile and rattled out a rhythm. Then he said, "Don't worry about her. She has gone off with a man, but she is not very far. She is getting homesick already, and next week, she will come home." All was well. The story of the daughter's absence would end with her safe return.

After the woman sat down, one of Don Pedro's neighbors said he saw a light in the sky. Another agreed and pointed toward what he saw. I was facing them. At first I did not bother to turn around. Sitting beside me, José Li Ning wore a skeptical expression and Lucile Loeser smiled. "There is a light, over there!" the *alzador* insisted. I turned, to be polite, and scanned the sky. Over the trees there was an unmistakable red glow. At first I was astonished, then, remembering my drink from the can of psychoactive cactus, I wondered if I was hallucinating. But the others saw it too. Were we having a collective hallucination? Fernando, Don Pedro's nephew, snorted: "That's where we're cooking the bricks!"

It was Don Pedro's turn before the *mesa*. He drank from the oyster shell through each nostril. He held a sword that vibrated, according to Calderón. He spoke about relatives who were jealous of him, who wanted to harm him. Suddenly, Calderón silenced him. "Your uncle the *brujo* has spotted us," he said. "He knows we're working tonight. I can see his light, although it is far off. It is coming toward us. You had better sit down."

Now it was my turn to stand before the *mesa*. Making a sacrifice for ethnography, I put the pointed shell up to my nose, bent backwards, and let its contents run through my nostrils. Once my convulsive belching stopped, I saw Calderón staring down to his left. "The sword of the Devil moves," he said dramatically. "Have you been baptized?" "No, I have not." "What is your religion?" "I am a Jew." "You bring the Devil with you!"

Without warning, the *brujo* spat rosewater across the mesa in a fine, strong spray, and threw a handful of small pebbles at my right shoulder. I was now baptized, Calderón explained. After proclaiming himself my godfather and the psychiatrist my godmother, he peered at his godson. "I see in the darkness hovering above your head a large clock: American time. It is always with you, dividing your mind into hours and minutes." "Is that an illness?" I asked, and Calderón laughed.

Sometime later, when the medical student and several others were sleeping, Calderón, who had been singing, abruptly stopped. He told Don Pedro to grab the cutlass at once and battle the evil *brujo*, his uncle, who was attacking the *mesa*. Holding the weapon over his head, the artist fell hard against the ground, grunting loudly, then rose and fell down hard again. Calderón ran to his side, took the cutlass in his right hand, and engaged in an energetic swordfight with an unseen assailant. The action was barely visible from the *mesa*, but the stomping of feet, the whirring blade, the grunting and thuds as Azabache hit the ground awoke everyone. Suddenly, a tense silence. Calderón strode back to the *mesa* and thrust the weapon into its place, not needing to mention that he had vanquished the jealous uncle's spirit.

Soon thereafter, Calderón spat rosewater three times at the *mesa*. We participants took turns standing before the *mesa* and rubbing ourselves down with a sword while the *brujo* sprayed rosewater on us three times each. Once that was done, he took the sword and swung it upward, spewing at it as if cleansing the sky. He did that three times. After he and his assistant bundled up the ritual paraphernalia, Calderón took up the sword of Christ and drew a cross on the ground where the *mesa* had been.

"*¿Qué horas son?*" Almost four in the morning.

Eduardo Calderón's parents migrated to Trujillo from the Cajabamba region in the Andes. His father was a handyman. As a child, Eduardo worked with wood, leather, ceramics, and metals, helping his father make shoes and fix all sorts of things. He also carried goods in the market, sold chocolates on the streets, and butchered animals at the slaughterhouse. In doing this work, the boy developed a rapport with people of all walks of life. On solo adventures, young Eduardo explored the desert and mountains near Trujillo, collecting shards and other treasures near pre-Incaic ruins. Those experiences ignited his curiosity, and he wondered about people in other lands, in other times.

"During my youth from more or less the age of seven or eight years," Calderón told the anthropologist Douglas Sharon, "I had some rare dreams. I still remember them. I remember dreams in which I flew, that my ego departed from the state in which it was, and I went to strange places in the form of a spiral. Or I flew in a vertiginous manner: Ssssssss, I departed. I tried to retain myself and I could not."

When Eduardo was seventeen and ready for high school, he enrolled, like Pedro Azabache, in the Catholic seminary, which offered a better education than the public schools. At seminary, he felt a calling to help people who were suffering and thought of becoming a priest. Eduardo began to read widely in philosophy, theology, and literature; he studied medicine and archaeology; and later in life, he learned about world religions via a Rosicrucian correspondence course.

During vacations, Eduardo went to Chimbote, a port city, where he worked in the fishing industry. He was strong, having taken up weight-lifting, and confident by nature. But on the waterfront, the gregarious young man got into trouble. Scars from a switchblade gave him lasting memories of a fight he entered unarmed.

At the end of seminary studies, Calderón went to Lima to take part in the national weightlifting championships as captain of Trujillo's gymnastic club team. He decided to stay in the city. By day, he worked with an uncle laying bricks; at night, he attended the School of Fine Arts. "I didn't like what they wanted to do with me," he told an interviewer in 1965. "The study of art was too pretentious and rigid. No one can be taught to be an artist. I preferred to return to my home."

That is not the whole story. Calderón had another reason to leave Lima. He had married an art school classmate. But her parents, appalled by his poverty, broke up the marriage and sent their daughter to live with relatives. It was after he failed to find her that the art school dropout returned north.

When he got back to Trujillo, said Calderón, "eruptions like volcanoes that did not emit pus broke out all over my body." He could not stand up; he lost his strength. His family decided to take him to a healer; both of his grandfathers had been *curanderos*. "Frankly, I didn't believe in those things," he recounted. But after he visited an herbalist and drank a brew Doña Laura had prepared, he recovered. That experience interested him in learning *curanderismo*.

Calderón took up fishing, casting his net from a one-man reed boat. He and María, a fisherman's daughter who had been his sweetheart when they were teens, began to live together. When Eduardo felt the restlessness that disturbed him in Lima when he fell ill, María took him to the *mesa* of an uncle who was a well-known healer. Eduardo began an apprenticeship with him. During one *mesa*, he told Sharon, "Christ called me. He said to me, 'Come here.' And He had me take the rattle and the dagger in my hands and sit in the place of the maestro. And the *curandero*'s assistants realized that the account pulled me. In other words, this was the initiation—the supreme instance in which the Divine Judge pulled me."

After that experience, Don Eduardo worked with *curanderos* in the north of Peru, gaining more knowledge. But he did not practice on his own until asked to do so by an uncle whose daughter was bewitched. "This girl couldn't look at mirrors because she saw the Devil there; she saw animals, she saw monsters, and a series of things. It seems as if they had worked on her hair, a common thing in witchcraft. Then in Chicama I placed two *mesas* for my cousin and cured her. That is where I began."[2]

Having learned the *curanderos'* art, Calderón promised himself "to serve man without thought of gain." It was as a fisherman that he made a living, traveling with María to Chimbote during the fishing season. He worked as a stevedore on the docks of Salaverry during the off-season. And he did sculpture in wood and clay. María was also a ceramist. Together they began making pots and babies. By 1964, when Calderón brought his *mesa* to the home of Pedro Azabache, they had ten children.

❀

Calderón's *mesa* elicits stories of private experience where they can be seen and heard by others, an appearance in the world that confirms their reality. Its physical layout reveals a dynamic field of symbolic figures. Vertically, there are swords and staffs representing beings that range from the Devil to Jesus Christ. Sculpted on stakes planted in the ground between them are animal spirits including Swordfish, Greyhound, and Eagle (ocean, land, and sky); the serpent staff of Moses; and various saints. Horizontally, the symbolic objects on the mesa are divided into three sections: a positive zone (symbols of Christianity and healing), a negative one (symbols of nature and sorcery), and a mediating strip between them (vision, wisdom, and the Sun). All of these objects are on the same level. There is nothing that does not meet the eye.

The field of symbols that comprise the *mesa* is like an instrument on which the healer plays, and the all-night ceremony, or performance, is part of a therapeutic process that goes beyond the space and time of the *mesa* itself. A documentary about Calderón, *Eduardo the Healer,* by Douglas Sharon with Kaye Sharon and Richard Cowan, presents his *curanderismo* in this larger context.

Above all, it shows the engaging personality of the man. We hear him whistling a waltz as he makes a Mochica-style pot; we see him with his family having breakfast; we listen as he explains his philosophy. Witches don't fly, says Calderón, "It's the mind that flies." He doesn't believe in magic or the supernatural: "God is the cosmic energy within ourselves." The film shows his diagnosis of a woman as he places a live guinea pig on her body, kills it, and examines the inner organs. We drive with him in a *colectivo* to Trujillo. In the market the healer buys medicinal herbs from the woman who cured him of a hex when he was lovesick at seventeen. "Because of me, you exist," says Doña Laura. The hour-long ethnographic film culminates in a *mesa* for Luciano Asmat, a man who had "a series of failures in his business and his home." The story that emerges from the *mesa* for Asmat helps the patient come to terms with his life.

Medicine stories have been performed in Peru for thousands of years. Although its history has been lost to living memory, ancient images of shamanic healing and present-day arrangements of objects on the *mesa* itself tell the secret of its survival in spite of threats and challenges posed by colonial conquest, religious opposition, and modern medicine.

Portraits of *brujos* rest among thousands of ceramic sculptures in archaeology museums. They wear turbans, wield rattles, hold potions, and touch patients who lie before them. Some sit staring in front of a horizontal space—a *mesa* by some other, long-lost name—with a stalk of the six-sided cactus San Pedro at their side.

Undoubtedly, the conquest of Peru had a devastating impact on *brujeria,* yet its techniques for healing, harming, and protecting people from harm survived. That may have been possible only in the northern Andes, far from the mines and *encomienda* lands where slave labor generated wealth for Spain. Even so, *brujeria* might not have survived the epidemics that depopulated indigenous communities in the sixteenth century and the antisorcery campaigns conducted by the Catholic Church in the seventeenth. Yet evidently, this tradition continued secretly at night beyond the reach of Spanish domination so that it could be revived openly later on, much as the potlatch of the Pacific Northwest and the world renewal ceremonies of the Klamath River tribes reemerged after generations of suppression in North America.

While the *mesa* lived on, it changed in important ways. The shaman's song, now sung in Spanish, lights a different path from the one the ancients traveled, although the seven mountains it invokes may be the same. San Pedro was ingested then and now, but some medicinal plants of the past no longer exist in Peru, and some plants used today for healing were not available before Pizarro.

To an extent, the objects on Calderón's *mesa* are the contemporary equivalents of ancient artifacts, many of which are buried in the sands of Peru's north coast, a desert that has preserved houses and temples, masks and murals, jewelry, textiles, and ceramics over the centuries. In 1965, when Calderón, then thirty-five, was restoring murals along the walls of Chan Chan, he showed a sorcerer's kit that had been found nearby to a new friend, Douglas Sharon, who was then an explorer. It contained "a set of stones of various sizes and shapes," wrote Sharon, whose apprenticeship with Calderón would launch his career as an anthropologist. "Eduardo laid them all out on a table and explained their functions and significance. He said that they corresponded to many of the personal artifacts laid out on his *mesa*."

Post-conquest contributions to the *mesa* such as the sword of Christ are obvious. Less evident is the organization of objects there, but it deserves attention; for that arrangement of things reveals both the strategy for survival of post-conquest *brujos* and a secret of their success in healing psychological disorders.

Throughout Latin America, the Catholic Church has harvested souls by absorbing elements of indigenous ritual into its ceremonies. Peruvian *brujeria* does the opposite, incorporating symbols of Christian belief into the *mesa*. In this way, healers can show that they are doing white magic; they are on the side of the angels. But white magic is codependent with black magic, the sorcery it defends against. Although an alliance between priests who persecuted sorcerers and sorcerers who were, or claimed to be, Christians is not in the historical record, something of the sort must have occurred. Witchcraft was the best weapon shamans had. To prevent the destruction of their way of life, they attacked Indians who sided with the Spanish. Missionaries could not have known how to protect Indians within their fold from sorcery. It took sorcery to fight sorcery. *Brujos* came forward as *curanderos*, or practitioners of white magic, to save the souls of people who believed in sorcery.[3]

This conflict is visible on the *mesa*. Unlike the vertical polarity of good and evil in Christian mythology, with the good souls going up to heaven and the evil souls condemned to hell, the shaman's sacred ground is horizontal. There, symbols of good and symbols of evil contend in dynamic tension with each other. Christian symbols dominate the zone of virtue, accompanied by crystals, sugar, and perfume. Indigenous symbols fill the negative zone. That is where the deer's foot, shards of ancient ceramics, shells, and packets of earth go. Separating the two is a narrow row lined with its own symbolic objects. These include a bronze disc representing the Sun, a deck of divining cards, and a glass jar containing magic herbs. As the sword of Christ and Satan's bayonet define the camps of good and evil, the serpent staff of Moses stands at the head of the in-between zone, mediating between the contending forces.

Healing power comes from the representation of all sides of the conflict on the *mesa* space. That spatial organization corresponds to the ritualization of the conflict during the time that the *mesa* is active. Instead of suppressing one side in favor of the other, the events that occur as the *mesa* unfolds, like the *brujo's* attack on Don Pedro, dramatize conflict, relieving stress and creating a sense of resolution. The *mesa*, in other words, is a symbolic microcosm that brings good and evil into a specific location within a short span of time to address a patient's particular affliction. It is comprehensive and comprehending.

The healer's role is crucial, for it takes talent to apply the power of the *mesa* to each patient's needs. In playing this part, Calderón was both showman and shaman. Unlike a Western psychotherapist, he performed in front of an audience: the people who attended the *mesa* to help the principal patient. Preceding each *mesa* was a diagnostic session aided by an eviscerated guinea pig. During the diagnosis, the healer, like any doctor, may observe signs of disease and distress; and he or she may learn directly from the patient what is wrong. But during the *mesa*, the problem is divined as an apparition beside that person. Sharing the vision with everyone present gives it the power of social recognition. The woman whose daughter ran away was able to express her distress instead of suffering in silence, and having others know her problem gave her the strength of a caring community. Calderón may well have known, through his wide social network, exactly where her daughter was and who she was with. As for his assurance that the girl would return the following week, whether that proved true or not, it surely relieved the mother's anxiety. It is through the *mesa* that the most private of experiences—physical pain and mental anguish—enter the world. For those who bring their affliction into the context of a healing ritual that others witness, that suffering means something.

Curanderos respond to physical and psychological ailments with medicinal plants as well as the *mesa*. For illnesses he lacked the ability to treat, Calderón referred patients to medical specialists or sent them to hospitals. To make those judgments required knowledge, and Calderón continually learned about anatomy, disease, and Western medicine. He knew some Chinese medicine as well. His friends called him "Chino."

Calderón's *mesas* expressed a vision of time and space, of the sacred and the profane, which drew from pre-Columbian and Christian sources. His *mesas* were artistic expressions as well, from the staffs he carved to the music he whistled, rattled, and sang.

I sensed a kinship between the artist and the shaman, between the painter who saw the beauty in every heart and the healer who eased the suffering of those who faced him in the dark. Before art, science, religion, and medicine became separate fields, they had a common ground. The diversity of shamanic expression from Siberia to South America is vast, but a fusion of religion and art, knowledge and healing power, characterizes shamanism everywhere.[4]

Another common denominator is fundamental: the shaman engages the attention of a group. The result is shared awareness. For cultural activities like theater and the movies, whose storytelling strategies derive from theater, this precondition reaches back to their common source in a pre-Socratic, prehistoric time. The Greek words for "theater" and "theory" stem from *theáomai*, which means to observe intently and grasp the significance of what one sees. Besides the sense of wonder awakened by nature, which is the experiential root of scientific knowledge, *theáomai* characterizes revelations that occur in ceremonies like the Dionysian rites, an antecedent of Western theater, and it could apply as well to the kind of attention leading to a sense of wholeness and renewal that a *mesa* inspires in its participants.

◌

The first documentary portrayed an indigenous people for whom shamanism aided the hunt and healed the sick. When a prospector for iron ore in Inuit country, Robert J. Flaherty, combined the revelatory power of photography with the art of storytelling, nonfiction filmmaking came into the world.

The earliest moving pictures, screened by the Lumière brothers in 1895, were slices of life: workers leaving a factory, a train entering a station. Called *actualités*, those brief films captured whatever appeared before the Lumières' lens. They were not documentaries. In 1913, when Flaherty carried a hand-cranked Bell & Howell movie camera to Canada's Hudson Bay Territory, he shot *actualités* of Inuits whose lives fascinated him and whose art he admired. According to Richard Meran Barsam, a historian of nonfiction film, the Inuit "taught Flaherty that art is more than just an expression of life's values, that it enables man to understand his relationship to life, and that it is also artifact, a utilitarian record of the moment."[5]

John Grierson, a pioneering theorist and promoter of nonfiction films, first used the term documentary in 1926 with reference to *Moana*, a movie by Flaherty. He defined it as the "creative treatment of actuality." However, Barsam's account of what Flaherty learned from his Inuit acquaintances comes closer to the mark. Unlike the *actualités* of today, brief videos on the web that use music and other creative elements, documentaries represent what is happening and has happened in ways that enable audiences to understand their subjects. The principal creative element that conveys that understanding is storytelling.

Flaherty's discovery of documentary storytelling came from a combination of effort and accident. During his next expedition, Flaherty concentrated more on filmmaking than on prospecting. Back in Toronto, he was editing footage when a cigarette ignited scraps of the nitrate-based negative, starting a fire that burned his hands and destroyed thirty thousand feet of film. Flaherty realized that what he had lost was incoherent—"a scene of this and that, no relation, no thread of story or continuity whatever."[6] He decided to bring the camera back to northern Canada and focus it on one man and his family. His protagonist was Allakariallak, whom Flaherty named Nanook after a polar bear in Inuit mythology. His antagonist, conveyed by film as theater never could, is humanity's age-old adversary: the forces of nature. Nanook and his fellow Inuits had to stave off starvation, survive dangers of the hunt, and stay warm during the long Arctic winter. *Nanook of the North*, which was released in 1922, showed that filmmakers can effectively and successfully use dramatic form in representing real-life subjects.

Like shamanism, the art of documentary employs magic to achieve its effects. It brings light where there is darkness, and it brings the dead to life. Editing creates conversations that never occurred and instantaneous moves from one place to another. One can say, as Roger Ebert did, that *Nanook of the North* has an "authenticity that prevails over any complaints that some of the sequences were staged."[7] But every documentary's authenticity has to be weighed on the scales of its artistry. And of course the means whereby any film is distributed to its far-flung audiences, whether by broadcast, screening or streaming, exemplifies the adage that yesterday's magic is today's technology.

Calderón did not believe in magic. He knew that witches do not fly. He used magic—the divination of a guinea pig's entrails, the staging of a fight with an evil spirit—to heal patients. He used symbolic objects and storytelling to put their misery into a meaningful frame of reference. And he used the act of performing in front of an audience to actualize a community whose experience of shared reality alleviates the solitude of suffering.

The cultural matrix of shamanism combines artistry with knowledge and ethical purpose. Today, when doctors and directors, scientists and scholars, painters, politicians, and priests work within their separate disciplines, that matrix is typically ignored if not dismissed as esoteric and irrelevant. Yet artistic forms that generate shared awareness, however they mix imagination with observation and whatever technologies they employ, have the power, in these times as in times beyond recorded memory, to counteract harmful fantasies and enlarge our understanding.

ERIK H. ERIKSON

Unlike music, mathematics, and facts whose validity is certain, stories that represent reality often fail to bridge the chasms between people.

One chasm Erik H. Erikson traversed as a student of the human psyche separates indigenous cultures from contemporary civilization. When I told Erikson about the *curanderismo* of Eduardo Calderón, he replied that his work was similar: the psychoanalyst elicits and interprets patients' stories in ways that put their suffering into perspective.[1] Erikson did not consider his therapeutic practice superior to native forms of healing.

The humility of his response was grounded in experience. In 1940, visiting the mouth of the Klamath River with anthropologist Alfred L. Kroeber, the young psychoanalyst met a Yurok doctor, Fanny Flounder. Erikson would later write about her with a respect that belied the then common use of the word "primitive" to characterize and denigrate indigenous societies. While Erikson "could not claim to be her professional equal" when it came to Flounder's approach to Yurok somatic disorders, he found it "possible to exchange notes" with Flounder about psychotherapy for children.

The shaman told him that a grandmother speaks to the spirits her grandchild "sees" after dark. If the child seems disturbed nonetheless, the grandmother who lives next door is called upon to sing a healing song. If that doesn't work, a doctor may be hired to do a cure. Flounder described the treatment she gives a child in his or her living room, with the whole family present. "She smokes her pipe to 'get into her power.' Then, if necessary, the child is held down by mother and father while Fanny sucks the first 'pain' from above the child's navel."

On meeting Flounder, Erikson noted "an acute sense of gloom." It brought to mind a power dream Kroeber told him Flounder once had in which "she saw the sky rising and blood dripping off its edge."[2] Both the anthropologist and the psychoanalyst interpreted her dream in terms of Yurok cosmography. In this vision of reality, people live on a world disk that can lose its horizontal position, which makes the land vulnerable to catastrophic flooding. Whales recently seen within the river were signs that the world was tipping dangerously. That may have been what the shaman dreaded. But neither man took Yurok history into account in considering her imagery of a world overwhelmed.[3]

It is a history of genocide, like that of other California Indians, although some downriver Yurok families managed to remain continuously within their ancient village sites. But historical perspective did not fall within Kroeber's professional boundaries. The anthropology of his day was deliberately ahistorical, seeking to preserve what remained of indigenous cultures from the harmful impacts of the encroaching world. What that world did to the tribes was for another discipline to examine. But most historians relegated American Indians to the anthropologists, with the result that native people were objects of study, not subjects in history. No one told their story; they were presumed to have vanished, no longer to exist. For Erikson, who became known for exploring connections between history and the individual psyche, little or no historical information would have been available even had he looked for it. Then, as now, published accounts of the destruction of California Indians were few and hard to find. When Yurok parents refused to let him near their children, Erikson did not understand the fear that the sight of a tall, blond, blue-eyed white man instilled in a people whose children had been killed or taken away from them ever since the gold rush. His collegial conversation with Fanny Flounder could not dispel the legacy of violence and suspicion left in the wake of people who considered theirs a superior race guided by Manifest Destiny.

For Erikson, the study of the individual psyche and its role in history opened a path toward what he called "an all-human identity." Yet the divide between peoples victimized by conquest and conquerors sustained by a self-justifying ideology presents challenges for those who would foster understanding across that divide via nonfiction storytelling.

In the field that he initiated, psychohistory, Erikson analyzed the ways in which inner conflicts of historic figures like Martin Luther, Hitler, and Gandhi stoked their powers of leadership in response to the crises of their times. These studies are grounded in Erikson's developmental theory of the human lifecycle. The way in which he examines connections between a person's life and times, between an individual's psychology and the historical moment, must have given Erikson a mirror as well as a lens, for his "way of looking at things" throws light on his own life story.[4]

The man who clarified the ways in which a person's conflicts and accomplishments are related to his or her sense of identity was deeply troubled by the mystery of his own identity. Erik H. Erikson never knew who his father was.

Erikson was born to an unmarried Danish Jew in Frankfurt, Germany, in 1902. Two years later, his mother, Karla Abrahamsen, wed her baby's pediatrician, Theodor Homburger. They became engaged on the condition that Erik be told that Theodor was his biological father. But the blond, blue-eyed boy bore no resemblance to his stepfather. When Erik Homburger had a bar mitzvah, the children at the temple called him "the goy." He came to believe that his real father was a Dane named Erik, yet he had no proof, and even after 1942, when Karla was widowed, she refused to tell him what he longed to know.

As a young man, Erik, like many of his generation, heeded Nietzsche's call to "become who you are." The teacher of an art school that Erikson attended encouraged artists to get to the essence of their subject, the artist's self. Self-creation and the experience of self became themes in a notebook Erikson kept as a young man. During his *wanderjahre* traveling aimlessly through Europe, he sketched strange, turbulent landscapes and disturbing portraits in black and white.

This "psychosocial moratorium," as Erikson would call the span of time when young adults float through life, unable to make commitments, culminated in his psychoanalytic training with Anna Freud and his marriage to Joan Serson. Erikson entered the Freudian circle by chance; he responded to a friend's letter that there was a job opening for a teacher in a school in Vienna that had been established for children of Sigmund Freud's patients. During his training analysis, which Anna Freud offered him, Erikson objected, "Look, I am an artist. This whole damn business is not for me." But Erikson came to understand "the artist in Freud." And Sigmund Freud's comment to his daughter about Erikson proved decisive: "Tell him he can help us make them (the public) *see*." Recalling this episode in his eighties, Erikson said, "That kind of thing can decide much of your identity."

Freud became a surrogate father for the fledgling psychoanalyst. With his love of art and highly visual imagination, Freud represented for the young man a synthesis of his own artistic way of seeing with the therapeutic calling his stepfather exemplified. "My identity with my stepfather," said Erikson, "only came out when I met Freud. Then I felt, now, to be that kind of doctor . . . well!"[5]

Erikson's psychoanalytic training occurred as Hitler was rising to power in Germany. Sensing the growing danger, Erik and Joan Erikson immigrated to the United States with their sons Kai and Jon in 1933. Like many US citizens, Erikson came to think of himself as a self-made man. "I made myself *Erik's son*," he wrote, after changing his name from Homburger to Erikson. "It is better to be your own originator."[6]

Erikson established a practice as a child analyst, using configurations of children's play as visual evidence of their psychological turmoil—a method he invented to compensate for lack of facility in English. Before long, he met intellectual leaders of his day, including the pediatrician Dr. Benjamin Spock, the anthropologists A. L. Kroeber and Margaret Mead, and Mead's husband, the philosophical biologist Gregory Bateson. Erikson soon made his mark with studies of American Indian childrearing, Hitler's youth, and Maxim Gorky's childhood, which he portrayed as a study of the Russian "national character."

During World War II, Erikson's examination of shell shock among veterans led him to formulate his concept of the identity crisis. As is often the case in the annals of healing, it was the absence of what healthy people take for granted that brought about its recognition. What impressed him most was "the loss in these men of a sense of identity." He thought "their lives no longer hung together—and never would again. There was a central disturbance of what I then started to call *ego identity*."[7]

Erikson was writing as a clinician; he observed the somatic symptoms as well as the outward circumstances of the trauma that afflicted these men. From a wider perspective, their inability to grasp the continuity of their lives can be described as a breakdown of the stories that gave them meaning and guided their actions.

The McCarthy era put Erikson's American identity to the test. Although he lacked academic credentials, Erikson received a full professorship in psychology at the University of California in Berkeley in 1949. Shortly thereafter, the administration added a loyalty oath to its annual contract: faculty were to pledge that they neither supported nor belonged to an organization that promoted "the overthrow of the United States." Although Erikson felt indebted to America and loyal to its government, he resented the oath and resigned his professorship.

Erikson was no friend of communism. It was his understanding of dictatorship and his fear of what "the McCarthy period might lead to" that made him take a stand against the anticommunist witch-hunt. In his essay "Wholeness and Totality," Erikson warned that McCarthyism bore the seeds of an American totalitarianism. By stereotyping the enemy, one separates the world into good vs. evil, us vs. them, thereby eliminating the potentiality for insight and reconciliation while opening the gates to the persecution of innocents. In contrast, Erikson hoped that within this nation of immigrants an "all-human identity" would grow as Americans "evolve a new world-image—an image which encompasses all of mankind."[8]

An embrace of the human family infused American culture during the postwar period, expressing an impulse to heal a divided world. The photographs that Edward Steichen displayed in New York City's Museum of Modern Art in 1955 under the heading "The Family of Man," with the aim of demonstrating "the essential oneness of mankind throughout the world," became the most popular exhibition in the history of photography. The impulse to experience this oneness took many forms, from the viewing of cinema from foreign lands in so-called art film theaters that sprang up around the country to world travel via jet planes. The idea that humanity is a global family contributed to the prominence in American popular culture of Margaret Mead and Erik H. Erikson, whose ideas became catchwords in innumerable conversations.

It was during this period, in the 1950s and '60s, that Erikson developed the concept of identity within the context of a theory of the human lifecycle. This theory is built on a Freudian foundation—the stages of development from infancy to early childhood—but goes beyond it in applying psychoanalytic thought to the entire lifespan. Erikson's lifecycle identifies eight stages of life, each with its own characteristic crisis. The crisis of young adulthood, for example, involves intimacy vs. isolation. The issue is not "does he get the girl or she the boy?" but "can they live with each other?" The crisis that the elderly face is a tension between a sense of integrity and despair: "did I fulfill myself or did I betray my potential?" The resolution of the crisis specific to each stage marks the transition to the next stage.

The issue of identity becomes critical during adolescence with its characteristic tension between identity formation and confusion, when young people become vulnerable to despair and suicide and also to the appeal of ideologies and organizations, like the military, that obviate individual will. But it is not set once and for all when the crisis is resolved. In Erikson's theory, "a sense of identity means a sense of being at one with oneself as one grows and develops."[9] Identity is affirmed in the intimacy of adulthood; in the generativity, with concern for emerging generations, of mature adults; and in the integrity of old age.

Erikson intended his theory to be scientific. In crafting it, he not only read medical and psychological research on human physical and emotional development, he also studied ethology, the science of animal behavior. He wanted his theory to apply to human beings everywhere, just as the theory of gravity applies universally to every body; but as an artist he also knew that what he had to offer was "a way of looking at things." To some extent, the lifecycle theory is a work of art, like Jacques' "seven ages of man" speech in *As You Like It*. And like great art, his theory, including the concept of identity, expresses an enduring truth.

For dramatists and storytellers, Erikson's stages of the lifecycle point to critical conflicts and choices that people face at defining moments in their lives. Identity, an issue that comes of age with adolescence, has unmatched drama. For it is then that one may lack a course of action in the midst of conflict. Until the point of view that an inner narrative provides is resolved, a person's character does not form sufficiently to exercise will in the service of an overarching storyline.

The identity of each individual draws from a range of experiences. An orphan may have no idea who she is or is meant to be. A boy who feels he is nobody may sacrifice the uniqueness of *who* he is for an identity based on *what* he is, which could be defined by his race, a disability, or his neighborhood gang. A girl born into a traditional family, whether tribal, dynastic, or religious, may enter a well-established place in the world with a predetermined way of living. In such cases, it is common to think that identity is a fixed characteristic. But identity is developmental, a work-in-progress. While inner conflict concerning identity can remain unresolved for years in a "psychosocial moratorium," it can also determine from a young age the course of a life. And the course of a life can change the course of history.

Erikson's books *Young Man Luther* and *Gandhi's Truth* demonstrate the value of psychoanalytic thinking about individual lives for the study of history. As a young man, Martin Luther suffered a severe identity crisis. Erikson's account of that crisis as an antecedent of Luther's dominance as a religious leader provides insights into the ideological compulsion that affected Europeans during the rise of totalitarianism, and Americans during the McCarthy era. "Ideological leaders, so it seems, are subject to excessive fears which they can master only by reshaping the thoughts of their contemporaries; while those contemporaries are always glad to have their thoughts shaped by those who so desperately care to do so."[10]

Erikson's notion that a "born leader" has a psychological crisis that brings to consciousness the inner conflicts of his contemporaries applies to Erikson's phenomenal popularity as "the father of the identity crisis" in the 1960s.

Disturbed youth emerged as a theme in American culture during the 1950s and early '60s. *Rebel Without a Cause*, a book by psychiatrist Robert Lindner, became a popular film in 1955. Paul Goodman's influential book *Growing Up Absurd* was published in 1960. *West Side Story*, a musical whose teenage characters are "depraved on accounta we're deprived," hit Broadway in 1961. "What is troubling the youth?" was a question on many minds, whether the young people referred to were urban gang members or college students.

Erikson's greatest appeal was among members of the "war baby" and "boomer" generations. Both generations came of age during a time when there were many career choices open to young people. The prosperity of the fifties and sixties meant that middle- and upper-middle-class youth did not have to worry about getting jobs; they had the luxury of "being themselves." But how does one become who one is? By what criteria does a person come to know his or her identity? In response, Erikson often quoted William James, who wrote of those times when a person feels "most deeply and intensely active and alive." Following this guideline, some young people decided to put their "own thing" above all else.

Erikson's concept of identity became invaluable during the sixties when the Cuban Missile Crisis made nuclear war suddenly seem imminent. With the potential that events would impose a shared fate on millions of people, their lives ending on short notice for no good reason, how should they live and what did it matter? No sooner did the urgency of that crisis wane than the Vietnam War forced a fateful choice upon young men: whether to avoid the draft through deferments, deceptions, or flight to Canada; to resist induction via the courts and direct action, risking imprisonment; or to join the military. These were formative decisions for people who came of age in the sixties. Many initiated careers and made political commitments as matters of life and death. Under these circumstances, a wisdom figure who understood the inner turbulence of youth and who gave it a name, the identity crisis, helped many come to terms with how they felt and indeed, with who they were.

During the sixties and seventies, Erikson became Harvard's most popular professor. His course on the human lifecycle was known among undergraduates as "From Womb to Tomb" and "From Bust to Dust." By the mid-sixties, one quarter of the senior class was enrolled in that course. At times, fire marshals had to clear the aisles and exits of the lecture hall.

Known as the leading psychoanalyst in America, Erikson appeared on the covers of the *New York Times Magazine* and *Psychology Today*. Jacqueline Kennedy asked him to help her children cope with the death of their father. Edward Kennedy sought his counsel on the psychological implications of running for president. Erikson met Black Panther Party leader Huey P. Newton to examine racism in America. When he came to Washington, DC, in 1973 to give a National Endowment for the Humanities lecture on Thomas Jefferson and the American Identity, Nixon's State Department held a black-tie reception and dinner in his honor. He was an intellectual celebrity.

Erikson himself sought guidance from a spiritual rather than a therapeutic source. During the sixties, the analyst traveled to India to write about what Mahatma Gandhi called the power of truth—*satyagraha*: the willingness to act nonviolently on behalf of one's own convictions without invalidating the truth others live by. For Erikson, Gandhi's insistence on responding to adversaries in human terms counteracted "a pseudo-species mentality" in which tribes, ethnic groups, and nations tend to regard themselves as *the* people at the center of the universe. Having this "firm sense of distinct and superior identity," *the* people regard others as evil or less than human and speak of them as if they were animals, lacking souls or lives with inherent value.[11] This refusal to acknowledge the humanity of the Other arises, in Erikson's analysis, from a fissure within the individual psyche: "The divided self is the counterpart of the divided species." Unconsciously, one sees in the Other "everything that's bad, including what's bad in oneself."[12] It is this lack of a human identity, Erikson thought, that enables nations to wage total war and to prepare for the thermonuclear annihilation of millions of people.

When *Gandhi's Truth* won both the Pulitzer Prize and the National Book Award, Erikson reached the height of his career. He took on a prophetic tone as he wrote and lectured about Gandhi, saying that "truth in Gandhi's sense points to the next step of man's realization of man as one all-human species, and thus to our only chance to transcend what we are."[13]

But as Erikson's fame increased, so did criticism of his work and of his failure to speak about the issues of the day. His long-time colleague Robert Jay Lifton was among those who insisted that Erikson take a stand against the Vietnam War. For Lifton, to speak truth to power is the responsibility of the intellectual, and Erikson's prominence made his responsibility all the greater. But Erikson refused to do so, claiming that it was inappropriate for an émigré like himself to take a stand on an issue of that kind, especially after his public refusal to sign a loyalty oath.

As the inclusive civil rights and antiwar movements of the sixties gave way to identity politics in the seventies, Erikson's theory of the lifecycle was challenged on several fronts. Carol Gilligan and Nancy Chodorow were among the feminist scholars who thought that his "eight stages of man" did not match the experience of women. They argued that the growth of girls occurs within a nexus of relationships more than is generally the case for boys, and there are discontinuities in the lives of women that do not characterize the development of men; for example, disruptions of their work lives in order to raise children. Yet while Erikson blurred *la diférence* between male and female in his lifecycle theory, he also came under fire for describing what seemed to be an essential difference between the sexes in an essay about patterns of play. Erikson's sketches, which accompany that essay, illustrated his thesis that girls favor inward-looking sheltered structures while boys enjoy thrusting outward into unbounded spaces. Most damaging of all, Marshall Berman attacked Erikson in the *New York Times Book Review* for hiding his own identity—his Jewishness. Asserting that the analyst "cannot bear to say: that he is a Jew," Berman accused Erikson of inauthenticity. For the analyst to strike a pose of universality while evading his particularity was no less than *"cosmic chutzpah."*[14]

For Erikson, it was not a matter of either/or. Within his layers of identity there was no essential definition. His biographer Lawrence J. Friedman spoke about this in an interview for my documentary about Erikson. "The Jewish community would say, 'You're a goy, you're a Gentile.' The Gentile community would say, 'You're a Jew.'" Robert Jay Lifton recalled asking him, "'Erik, are you a Jew or a Gentile?' And he would say, 'Why, both of course.'"

The question of Erikson's Jewish identity was an obvious one to ask the psychoanalyst. Here was a man with a Jewish upbringing who married an Episcopalian and whose major works examined Gentile spiritual leaders, including Martin Luther, a German whose antisemitic writings spurred the destruction of Jewish homes and synagogues. But Erikson's answer to Lifton's question was too ambiguous to have quelled the controversy over his identity, and a simple answer would have belied his understanding of identity as a complex developmental process in which ethnic identity need not submerge a unique sense of self nor one's responsibility as a human being. Erikson chose not to respond in public to Berman's attack even as sales of his books plummeted and many who had respected him concluded that his image was a false front. Although friends defended him and Margaret Mead proclaimed him "one of the greatest men in the world," he lost his influence and much of his reputation. The Eriksons returned to California where Erik wrote about—and lived—the last stage of the lifecycle: old age.

☾

Erikson traveled far from the Freudian shores. Freud's European outlook was pessimistic. He sought to convert patients' miseries into "common unhappiness." Erikson, with an optimism that suited many Americans, regarded the healthy course of a human life cycle as a succession of strengths, going from basic trust in infancy through identity in adolescence and the intimacy of young adulthood toward the integrity of old age. It was a radical departure for Erikson to use the Freudian stages of psychosexual development, which genital arousal in puberty completes, as the foundation for a lifelong theory of psychosocial growth. In doing so, he dethroned the Oedipus story as the template for conflicts within the psyche. Whatever unconscious desires a child may have to marry one parent and kill the other, that complex hardly determines whether a mature adult achieves the strength of generativity or declines into a state of stagnation, or whether one feels despair in old age instead of a sense of integrity. Yet in spite of his departures from Freud's theory, the man who searched in vain for his Danish father never rejected his German Jewish father figure.

Erikson was not alone in removing the Oedipus story from center stage as the dramatic arc of psychodynamics. Other analysts, including Nancy Chodorow, have criticized Freud's emphasis on that one myth. However, the inspiration Freud received from Sophocles' *Oedipus Rex* went beyond the plot of that play. An avid student of literature, Freud saw the cathartic power of Greek tragedy as a model for what analysis can accomplish. It is the recognition of reality—Agave's realization that she killed her son no less than Oedipus's facing the truth of his life and blinding himself once he *sees*—that awakens tragic awareness. The replacement of illusion with recognition of reality in tragic drama prefigured Freud's therapeutic goal: "Where id was, let ego be." Whether it is the unconscious that gets revealed rather than "a divinity that shapes our ends, rough hew them how we may," as Hamlet said, or whether the desired outcome is common unhappiness or realization of a strength corresponding to one's stage in the lifecycle, the courage to face reality facilitates healing.

Erikson's bust-to-dust theory of the lifecycle recognized the importance of storytelling in human development. "To be an adult," he wrote, "means among other things to see one's life in continuous perspective, both in retrospect and in prospect. By accepting some definition as to who he is, usually on the basis of a function in an economy, a place in the sequence of generations, and a status in the structure of society, the adult is able to selectively reconstruct his past in such a way that step for step, it seems to have planned him, or better, he seems to have planned *it*."[15] In contrast, the "psychoneurotic casualties" of World War II whose condition Erikson analyzed in terms of the clash between identity and confusion, lost "the ability to experience one's self as something that has continuity and sameness, and to act accordingly."

Healing required reconstruction "of the patient's family history and of those changes in his social life which receive meaning from and give meaning to his . . . ego development."[16]

Writing *Gandhi's Truth*, Erikson brought psychoanalytic awareness of the subjective relationship between analyst and patient into historical storytelling. He addressed a chapter to the Mahatma, critiquing Gandhi's self-interpretation in his autobiography, *The Story of My Experiments with Truth*, as well as his cruelty toward his wife and "patriarchal bad manners" in relation to their son Harilal. Erikson's purpose was not to accuse his subject or to make a clinical judgment. He realized that coming to terms with Gandhi required self-awareness of his response to the man he was writing about. Like Freud, who analyzed his dreams in developing psychoanalysis, and like Gandhi, who probed his motivations in writing the autobiography, Erikson knew that insight into another begins in oneself, that there is a relativity of truth wherein the relationship between a narrator or analyst and his or her subject is a crucial factor.

One factor in that relationship is the degree of distance between the person who tells the story and the person it's about. That ranged, in Erikson's case, from his study of Martin Luther, a fervent anti-semite separated by centuries if not by language from the analyst, to his biographical essay about Freud. How does one find the right perspective to overcome too great a distance, on the one hand, and too close a kinship, on the other, to have a valid understanding of one's subject that is worth sharing with countless others?

A key question for those who choose a subject for nonfiction story-telling is, what are their motivations for initiating this work? Guiding Erikson through his study of Gandhi was the idea that *satyagraha*, like psychoanalysis, "amounts to a truth method"[17]; that they are comple-mentary disciplines, with one expressed in confrontational action and the other in candid speech; and that their convergence in the twentieth century "may well be of historical, if not evolutionary, significance."

This assertion raises another question for those who would tell true stories: what is your truth method?

GINETTA SAGAN

Once a man asked me to make a documentary about his mother. Not
having heard of her, I was skeptical. However much Loring Sagan
admired his mother, he lacked the distance to evaluate whether multitudes of diverse strangers would find her worthy of their attention.
Then too came the problem of getting a film funded, produced, and
screened when its subject was not well known, along with the question
of whether this project was a productive use of my time. But a fellow
filmmaker, our mutual friend Gail Evenari, had recommended I meet
Loring, and soon I realized that his mother was someone I too admired
and wanted the world to know.

Ginetta Sagan was the human rights campaigner who made Amnesty
International an organization that effectively defends the rights of prisoners of conscience in countries around the world. Amnesty does this
by publicizing their stories and encouraging its members to write on
their behalf. Sagan herself was a storyteller. Her personal stories, in
addition to the accounts circulated by Amnesty, throw light on people
punished for their beliefs and hidden behind bars.[1]

Sagan was incognito from the day she was born. The love child of
a French Jewish doctor and a married Italian Catholic doctor, Ginetta
took on the identity of her wet nurse's baby who had died two years
earlier. This arrangement shielded her parents from scandal—her father,
under Italian law, was unable to obtain a divorce—and it protected
Sagan from persecution as a Jew during the war years.

Growing up with a false identity also prepared Sagan for her role in
the Italian Resistance. Known as Topolino, or "little mouse," the four-
foot-eleven teenager seemed innocuous. The prominent Fascist officer
and his mother for whom she worked as a maid in 1943 never guessed
that as the girl scrubbed every surface of the house, she was listening
in on phone conversations and searching for official documents in the
trash.

Sagan's branch of the *Resistenza*, based in Milan, succeeded in smuggling nearly ten thousand people into Switzerland. According to Sagan,

Topolino personally escorted three hundred anti-Fascists, Jews, and draft evaders across a barbed wire fence that marked the Swiss border. The piece of barbed wire she retrieved after the war and wrapped around a candle would become a symbol of Amnesty International.

In February 1945, Topolino was captured, imprisoned, and raped. One night she was sitting alone in a pitch-black jail when "a man threw a loaf of bread in the cell, calling [her] a whore and all sorts of names." Hidden inside the hollow loaf she found a matchbox containing one match and a tiny scrap of paper. Lighting the match, she read: "*Coraggio! Lavoriamo per te.*" (Courage! We are working for you.) "All the efforts the Fascists had expended trying to disintegrate my personality were overthrown in that moment."

Sagan told that story many times. She wanted people to know that they can make a difference by writing prisoners of conscience and their jailers, letting the former know that they are not alone and the latter that they are held responsible for what they do.

Creating an international constituency to insist that people in every country, regardless of their religion, politics, and ethnicity, have the right not to be persecuted or unjustly imprisoned became Sagan's lifework.

In 1967, a friend introduced Sagan to a Greek woman who described her experiences under the military junta. Sagan learned that methods of torture that the Gestapo used in wartime Italy and throughout occupied Europe were being practiced again. Shortly thereafter, she joined Amnesty International, which had been founded by London lawyer Peter Benenson in 1961.

Sagan applied the techniques of the Resistance to the task at hand. She formed a network that included veterans of the Italian underground and Greeks who were in hiding from the junta. Sagan compiled lists of prisoners and located the prisons where they were detained. Fact-finding required her to travel to Greece several times, always disguised and under an assumed name.

In 1971, Sagan recruited Joan Baez and Melina Mercouri to perform at a fundraising concert in support of the junta's prisoners. After this event, which drew 10,000 people to Berkeley's Greek Theatre, Baez and Mercouri joined a group on the Stanford campus that formed the first West Coast chapter of Amnesty International.

When General Pinochet overthrew President Allende's government and imprisoned thousands of Chileans opposed to the coup d'etat, Sagan somehow reached the general's direct phone line and demanded that he release them all. Subsequently, Sagan, Baez, and their West Coast cohort initiated Amnesty International's first direct mail campaign. Their efforts proved instrumental in expanding Amnesty's influence and its US membership.

A diminutive woman with a warm smile and intense energy, Sagan insisted that anyone could have done the same. Working out of her home, she seemed to be nothing more than "that housewife in Atherton," as former CIA chief William Casey once called her.

Alliance with celebrities did not diminish Sagan's passion for anonymity. She learned to hide within the shadow cast by the light of publicity.

In 1985, Sagan invited Baez to travel with her to Poland, which was then under martial law. Sagan had raised money to support people imprisoned for participation in Solidarity, the worker's revolution that, ironically, challenged the supposedly Marxist Soviet empire. How to get funds into Poland was her problem. When their flight arrived in Warsaw, Baez and the film crew that accompanied her became the focus of attention. Sagan, ostensibly just another member of the entourage, was smuggling thick wads of currency under her clothes. Suddenly her pantyhose snapped. Baez quickly took her friend's luggage and told customs officials that the woman's back was hurt. "I walked as if I had broken my spine," recalled Sagan.

Trying to remain incognito, Sagan accompanied the famous folksinger to Father Jankowski's parish house where they spent the night. The next day she hid in the church as Baez entertained the congregation.

The sixty-year-old smuggler managed to accomplish her mission, but her presence became known to the authorities. As she traveled in a car chauffeured by Lech Walesa's driver, the vehicle's brakes failed. Believing the car to have been sabotaged by agents of General Jaruzelski, Sagan made a point of posing for a photograph beside the wreck, a triumphant smile on her bloody face. She did not care that her name be known, but she wanted the general and his henchmen to see her spirit.

Making a film about Ginetta Sagan would show that spirit to the world.

When we met, she recognized me. I was certain I had never met her before but did not say so, not wanting to contradict her. Sagan was unlike anyone I had known: small enough to be called Topolino, she seemed relaxed in her Atherton ranch house yet highly alert, sizing me up. Sagan had shown the door to another man who wanted to make a documentary about her. Life was too short, she said, to educate him about twentieth-century European history.

I had some knowledge of that history. My concept was to make a double biography, pairing Sagan with Vaclav Havel, the playwright who at that time was President of the Czech Republic. Earlier, when Havel was imprisoned for his role in the Charter 77 campaign protesting his country's violations of human rights, Amnesty International declared him a prisoner of conscience. When Havel came to California for a visit, Sagan was one person he wanted to meet. Joan Baez invited them to her home. A shaky video of that gathering was available, enough to make a visual link for documentary storytelling purposes.

I advocated a double biography since many who never heard of Sagan admired Vaclav Havel; their interest in him could lead them to her. The drama of Havel's struggle in Czechoslovakia would complement the story of her worldwide campaign. His understanding of the need for individuals to "live within the truth"[2] within a system that would strip them of their integrity underscored the importance of supporting prisoners of conscience. His sense of "the power of the powerless" could help viewers appreciate Sagan's anonymity and understand that they themselves have the potential to be powerful.

As we spoke, Ginetta Sagan placed me. My cousin Vivian Scott had worked with her closely as a member of the West Coast chapter. But Vivian died more than a decade before I met Sagan. She may have seen me at the memorial service at Stanford among hundreds of Vivian's family members and friends. But how could she have remembered my face?

Over lunch in her backyard, Sagan explained. In the Resistance she was trained to recall everyone who had been near her. This was life-or-death knowledge. Someone she had seen before might be a spy, or a fascist she may need to finger, or an ally she could depend on. Looking through thousands of photographs helped her hone her memory. Still, I found it incredible that Sagan could have recognized me after all those years. Perhaps when I met her, a family resemblance brought Vivian to her mind.

The documentary about Sagan, called *Courage in a Matchbox*, was never made. Havel's wife did not allow an interview. He had presidential duties, and he was ill with chronic bronchitis; she guarded his time. Then Sagan died. She was seventy-five.

○

Just as Sagan sought to inspire human rights activists by telling stories of the Resistance, a biographical film about her had the potential to inspire a new generation. To be known beyond the reach of their deeds and influence, to be remembered after their days are done, actors in history need "the help of the artist, of poets and historiographers, of monument-builders or writers," wrote Hannah Arendt, "because without them the only product of their activity, the story they enact and tell, would not survive at all."[3]

The power of stories to keep actions alive over time illuminates the history of religions, of nations, of civil disobedience, and many other arenas, from sports to warfare, where exemplary deeds drive events. Edward Snowden told Daniel Ellsberg that what inspired him to risk imprisonment for releasing classified documents about National Security Agency surveillance was seeing a documentary about Ellsberg— *The Most Dangerous Man in America* (codirected by Judith Ehrlich and Rick Goldsmith). And what inspired Ellsberg to release the top-secret *Pentagon Papers* during the Vietnam War? In an interview with Ehrlich, he said it was hearing Randy Koehler, a member of the Resistance, speak about his impending imprisonment for draft refusal. In making his sacrifice, Koehler, in turn, drew inspiration from a tradition of civil disobedience reaching back through the civil rights movement to Gandhi's *satyagraha* campaigns, to the filling of jails by the Industrial Workers of the World, who recited the Declaration of Independence in cities where outdoor meetings were banned, to Thoreau's imprisonment for tax resistance in protest of slavery and the Mexican-American War.

For people to exercise their freedom, it is important to know what others have done in times past and to learn from their failures as well as their successes. It is crucial as well to understand the factors that foster conformity to injustice and tyranny and the forces that punish people who "live in truth." The conflict between dominators and those who refuse to submit to them is a never-exhausted source of stories that need to be told. It is a struggle, as Milan Kundera wrote, of "memory against forgetting."

⊞ Hannah Arendt

Stories make the world and stories limit it. Those who favor tales that support their identities and advance their ends while shunning or censoring all others maintain a fixed horizon—unless the unexpected breaks through those boundaries. For others, stories bring all kinds of people, situations, and knowledge into view—until events that have no precedent leave them in the dark, unable to grasp what has happened.

Telling stories of unprecedented events and, in doing so, seeking to understand them was a central concern of Hannah Arendt. "The quest for meaning," she wrote, ". . . is in no way different from men's need to tell the story of some happening they witnessed."[1] For her, the happening whose meaning she needed to grasp, above all, was totalitarianism and genocide.

"The most important thing for me," Arendt told an interviewer, "is to understand."[2] Many fail to understand her. Arendt's work does not fall into traditional categories. She wrote histories of revolution and of totalitarianism, but she was not a historian. She wrote about politics and forms of government but was not a political scientist. She critiqued philosophy and refused to call herself a philosopher. Instead, Arendt is widely regarded as the preeminent political thinker of the twentieth century. She was a storyteller as well, who once spoke of her work as "my old-fashioned storytelling."[3]

One story she told, and the way she told it, roused a hornet's nest of controversy. The attacks that her account of the trial of Adolph Eichmann stirred up did long-lasting damage to her reputation.

"This is the first time in fifty years," said Sandra Luft, in 2013, "when it is possible to have civil discourse about Hannah Arendt." With that hopeful remark, Luft, a professor of humanities at San Francisco State University, opened a discussion of *Eichmann in Jerusalem* at a synagogue in Berkeley.

What increased the odds for civil discourse was a feature film. Directed by Margarethe von Trotta, *Hannah Arendt* dramatizes the controversy concerning Arendt's report on the Eichmann trial, which was originally published in five issues of *The New Yorker* in 1963. Before the night of the discussion, Luft had circulated passages from the book and recommended that congregants view the film. Civil discourse did occur, and that meeting launched a reading group that has met monthly ever since to discuss Arendt's work.

During those fifty years between the Eichmann book and the biographical film, I experienced hostility directed at Arendt that ruled out conversation. Once, invited to a *shabbat* dinner at the home of the rabbi of my girlfriend at the time, I mentioned that I was a graduate student in the Committee on Social Thought at the University of Chicago and that I had come there to study with Arendt. The rabbi's response was so vitriolic that there was no rescuing the evening. Many years later, in Jerusalem, I browsed through a bookstore that seemed congenial. It had books in English as well as Hebrew. Upstairs, I found a couch and comfortable chairs facing a whiteboard: a place for meetings and conversation. The bookseller followed me upstairs and offered me a cup of coffee. I asked if he had any of Hannah Arendt's books. His face twisted into a grimace of contempt: "You mean Heidegger's *girlfriend*?" What a shame, I thought, that a Jewish bookstore would scorn a writer whose essays on Zionism include a prescient analysis of the challenges Israel has faced ever since its founding; whose book *The Origins of Totalitarianism* examines Hitler's and Stalin's unprecedented form of tyranny; a writer whose "literary existence," as she once said, had "the Jewish question as the focal point of my historical and political thinking."[4]

Reporting on the Eichmann trial was for Arendt a sequel to the study of totalitarianism, for it filled a gap in her understanding. "I would never be able to forgive myself," she wrote her former professor and lifelong friend Karl Jaspers, "if I didn't go and look at this walking disaster face to face in all his bizarre vacuousness, without the mediation of the printed word. Don't forget how early I left Germany and how little of all this I really experienced directly."[5]

Several aspects of Arendt's report triggered the assault on her reputation. One was her criticism of the trial. In a letter to Jaspers, Arendt defended Israel's right to put Eichmann on trial, even though to do so, its agents kidnapped the Nazi in Buenos Aires; even though Israel did not exist at the time of Eichmann's service to the German death-machine; even though there was no law on the books commensurate to his crime, which Arendt considered not just a crime against the Jewish people but a crime against humanity.[6] She did not, however, approve of a show trial, which, instead of judging Eichmann for his deeds, turned him into a symbol of the Holocaust and put history on trial, allowing many days of testimony that failed to mention him at all. She insisted that judgment be based on the specific acts of the accused. That conviction accounts for Arendt's response to the German reporter who, after a harrowing day of testimony, approached her and buried his face on her shoulder. "*Ach*, Hannah," he cried, "We are all guilty!" She pulled back and stared at the man. "And you?" she demanded, "What did *you* do?"[7]

A second controversial aspect of her report, which von Trotta's film emphasizes, involves an issue hardly mentioned in the trial. To Jaspers, Arendt expressed her concern that Eichmann's defense would reveal "to what a huge degree the Jews helped organize their own destruction. That is, of course, the naked truth, but this truth, if it is not really explained, could stir up more anti-Semitism than ten kidnappings."[8] The fact that Jewish leaders provided logistical support the Nazis needed, as documented in Raul Hillberg's *The Destruction of the European Jews*, had to be acknowledged, Arendt thought. Not only would withholding those facts provide ammunition to those who might challenge her account, not including them would prevent her readers from understanding what happened. So she reported: "The Jewish Council of Elders were informed by Eichmann or his men of how many Jews were needed to fill each train, and they made out the list of deportees. The Jews registered, filled out innumerable forms, answered pages and pages of questionnaires regarding their property so that it could be seized more easily; then they assembled at the collection points and boarded the trains." To Arendt, as a Jew, "this role of the Jewish leaders in the destruction of their own people is undoubtedly the darkest chapter of the whole dark story."[9] These sentences were to be widely and often willfully misinterpreted, as if Arendt, rather than clarifying what actually happened, were defending Eichmann, and as if the assistance Jewish leaders gave the Nazis were worse than the Holocaust itself.

Adding to the outrage was Arendt's account of Eichmann's character, or lack thereof—his "bizarre vacuousness." But that was what she encountered when she watched him face to face and when she read the transcript of his interrogation, which, incongruously, made her laugh. Here was a man whose mind was crammed with clichés and self-fabricated stock phrases. "The longer one listened to him," Arendt wrote, "the more obvious it became that his inability to speak was closely connected with an inability to think, namely to think from the standpoint of somebody else." What struck her so funny as she read the text of his police examination is that Eichmann talked "in the tone of someone who was sure of finding 'normal, human' sympathy for a hard-luck story."[10] He seemed oblivious of context, incapable of relating to the reality of his situation.

The astonishing discrepancy between the mediocrity of the man and the monstrosity of his deeds made Arendt question the common and comforting notion that evildoers are far from normal. On the contrary, evil emerges not from demonic depths but from shallow subservience. Eichmann was a bureaucrat, and bureaucracy she would later define as "rule by Nobody."[11] The discovery that the accused was not the villain people expected to hold responsible for the Holocaust, that instead he was a man who had no sense of responsibility at all, Arendt underscored with the subtitle of her book "A Report on the Banality of Evil." Not only did this conclusion deny that a modern-day pharaoh or Haman was to blame for the tragedy of the Jews, it had the horrifying implication that ordinary people can do extraordinary harm even in the absence of tyranny or totalitarian rule.

The rejection of Arendt's report was strong and widespread. "Funny: you said to me once that I tell people the truth so naïvely," Jaspers wrote her as the controversy over *Eichmann in Jerusalem* raged. "Now you have far exceeded me in that naïveté."[12]

Margarethe von Trotta's film dramatizes that controversy in various ways, ranging from the stack of hate mail Arendt received to confrontations with colleagues and the end of friendships. Not every scene portrayed in *Hannah Arendt* actually occurred, but as Albert Camus wrote, "Fiction is the lie through which we tell the truth." Other scenes and facts about the Eichmann episode that the film does not include are well documented in Arendt's correspondence and additional sources.

A defamation campaign against Arendt broke out even before the last of the *New Yorker* articles appeared in print. Leading the charge was the Anti-Defamation League. The ADL sent a letter to rabbis telling them to censure Arendt; and it circulated a bulletin outlining the book's controversial statements, a memorandum detailing its factual errors, and an article maligning Arendt, along with the recommendation that reviewers take these sources into account. One regional Jewish newspaper that rose to the occasion headlined its article, "Self-Hating Jewess Writes Pro-Eichmann Series." "The Jewish community is up in arms," Hans Morgenthau wrote Arendt, describing a meeting held by Hillel House at City College of New York. "Reality has protruded into the protective armor of illusion and the result is psychological havoc."[13]

Arendt originally dismissed the controversy as a tempest in a teacup, advising her husband, Heinrich Blücher, in a letter from Europe, "that one shouldn't pay any attention to it."[14] But four months later, after returning home, she wrote Jaspers, "I'm amazed and never expected anything like this, and I can see, too, that it's downright dangerous.

(People are resorting to any means to destroy my reputation. They have spent weeks trying to find something in my past that they can hang on me. They finally gave up, but are going at it differently now.) If I had known this would happen, I probably would have done precisely what I did do."[15]

Arendt's book about the Eichmann trial put her on trial. Arendt's description of his character made her a character in stories told by her adversaries. Although she never anticipated this drama, Arendt was well aware of the part she played. Indeed, in an essay about Jewish character types, she defined it. "The Jew as Pariah: A Hidden Tradition" describes Bernard Lazare, a French writer in the era of the Dreyfus Affair, as a "conscious pariah." Lazare, she wrote, made a "heroic effort to bring the Jewish question openly into the arena of politics."[16] Arendt, in her writings about Zionism prior to the establishment of Israel, called for direct political engagement between Jews and Arabs, and she opposed the essentialization of antisemitism and Jewish victim-hood, as if Jews, unlike every other people, "were not history-makers but history-sufferers, preserving a kind of eternal identity of goodness whose monotony was disturbed only by the equally monotonous chronicle of persecutions and pogroms."[17] Arendt's account of the Eichmann trial, which upset the unquestioned assumptions of Jewish goodness and Gentile fiendishness, made her the conscious pariah of her time.

Although Arendt made a sharp distinction between public and private, rejecting the feminist assertion that the personal is political, one needs a sense of her as a private person to understand her role in this controversy. Fortunately, the acting of Barbara Sukowa in a thoroughly researched, well-imagined work of fiction reveals the humanity of this demonized writer. We see Arendt as a *hausfrau* chopping cabbage; a hostess who argues passionately with her closest friends; a woman whose loving husband is an independent thinker like herself; a solitary smoker whose cigarette glow pierces the night like the headlight on a train of thought.

Seeing Arendt as a *mensch* takes the Eichmann book beyond the pages it is printed on and puts it into the context of her personal life. One of the distinctions Arendt made divided thinking from feeling. Everyone's emotions, she maintained, are alike, just like inner organs. It is by speaking their minds, especially in a public space, that people show who they uniquely are. Yet it is by portraying Arendt's emotions that the film *Hannah Arendt* reveals the depth underlying her public persona. A quality of the Eichmann book that alienated many readers is her use of irony, sarcasm, and paradox—a style Norman Podhoretz, in his *Commentary* review, called "the perversity of brilliance."[18] In the film he claims she is "all cleverness and no feeling." But a dramatic dialogue between Arendt and Blücher suggests the emotions that the book conceals. Blücher worries that Arendt's feelings could overwhelm her when facing the Holocaust at the Eichmann trial. He has reason for concern. Arendt recalls being imprisoned in Gurs, the detention camp in France from which she managed to escape before Eichmann transported its inhabitants to a death camp. Arendt encouraged the women who were her fellow prisoners. Then, she recounts, "one evening, I suddenly lost my courage. I was so tired. So tired I wanted to leave the world I so loved." Characteristically, when, later in the film, she speaks to her students about Gurs, Arendt is ironic, saying the Jews' enemies sent them to concentration camps, their friends to detention camps. But seeing her in this imagined scene with Blücher, we have a sense of the depths of despair Arendt literally came to terms with in writing *Eichmann in Jerusalem*. Her style, which appears to lack feeling, helped Arendt master the subject emotionally as well as factually. As she admitted in a letter to her friend, the novelist Mary McCarthy, "I wrote this book in a curious state of euphoria. And ever since I did it, I feel—after twenty years—light-hearted about the whole matter."[19]

Arendt wrote an essay, "Truth and Politics," in response to "the so-called controversy after the publication of *Eichmann in Jerusalem*." In it, she addresses "the question of whether it is always legitimate to tell the truth." Arendt concludes that "the political function of the story-teller—historian or novelist—is to teach acceptance of things as they are. Out of that acceptance, which can also be called truthfulness, arises the faculty of judgment." A narrator's truthfulness has a liberating effect. "To the extent that the teller of factual truth is also a storyteller, he brings about that 'reconciliation with reality' which Hegel . . . understood as the ultimate goal of all philosophical thought."[20] Yet reconciliation with the reality exposed at the Eichmann trial did not mean Arendt mastered the past itself. "We can no more master the past than we can undo it," she wrote the year before Eichmann was captured in Argentina. "But we can reconcile ourselves to it."[21]

The fact that it took a work of dramatic art to disclose otherwise unknowable aspects of her experience would not have surprised Arendt at all. She was well aware that one needs imagination to grasp reality. "Imagination alone," she wrote, "enables us to see things in their proper perspective."[22] And she was aware that she herself could not obtain a proper perspective regarding her own life. "What the storyteller narrates must necessarily be hidden from the actor himself," she maintained, "at least as long as he is in the act or caught in its consequences, because to him the meaningfulness of his act is not in the story that follows."[23] Only when an action has ended and become a story to be told can its meaning appear.

Arendt was not particularly interested in film as a mode of storytelling, but she had high regard for the revelatory power of drama. That was due in part to the public space that theater establishes. There people can assemble to witness representations of what interests them as citizens of the world. When spectators within a theater experience what is on stage as if it were real, they suspend judgment until the story has played out to the end. Their ability to judge arises out of the recognition of what has happened.

Beyond theater as a forum, the structure and content of dramatic representation mattered to Arendt. What audiences see on the stage of that public space are characters who act, who disclose who they are. Action is a central theme in Arendt's writings, for it embodies two fundamental aspects of the human condition as she describes it: natality, the fact that each generation and potentially each person brings something new into the world; and plurality, the multiplicity of people within the world. The disclosure of character, the plurality into which one acts, and the unpredictability of the outcome are the stuff of drama. And it is through dramatic storytelling that the evanescence of action, which has no permanent result in itself, is preserved for posterity. Arendt considered theater "the political art par excellence; only there is the political sphere of human life transposed into art. By the same token, it is the only art whose sole subject is man in his relationship with others."[24]

A playwright of the German Enlightenment, Gotthold Ephraim Lessing, influenced Arendt's thinking about the role of relationships in public life. In 1959, on accepting the Lessing Prize of the Free City of Hamburg, Arendt said that for Lessing, friendship has political importance, for it concerns "the common world, which remains 'inhuman' in a very literal sense unless it is constantly talked about by human beings," unless it becomes "the object of discourse." The common world, unlike the realm philosophers like Plato inhabit, has no room for *the* truth, for that would mean an end to discourse and to friendship. Instead, when people speak *their* truth, the result is a multiplicity of opinions, and those views, along with the speakers' stories, illuminate the world they have in common.

Like Lessing, instead of seeking "in the warmth of intimacy the substitute for that light and illumination which only the public realm can cast,"[25] Arendt and her friends discussed public affairs, and they did so with confidence that the bonds of friendship could withstand their differences of opinion. In his eulogy at her funeral service at Riverside Memorial Chapel in New York City in 1975, Hans Jonas spoke of

Arendt's "genius for friendship." Regarding her passion for discourse, he said, "She liked, of course, to be right and on occasion could be quite formidably contentious; but she did not believe, as she confided to me, that 'truth' is to be had for us these days. She believed, instead, in the incessant, always temporary trying for that face of it which the present condition happens to turn toward us. Thinking through is its own reward, for we will be more understanding after than we were before. We will have more light, and still not have 'the truth.'"[26]

In view of the importance of friendship for Arendt, the movie's depiction of conflict with Jonas and other close friends over the Eichmann book is both painful and problematic. Kurt Blumenfeld, whom she had known since she was twenty and he forty-two, was a leader of the Zionist Organization of Germany and Arendt's "mentor in politics" before he emigrated to Israel in 1933. The film depicts him greeting her warmly when she arrives to cover the trial; and, in a deathbed scene, it dramatizes his break with her over *Eichmann in Jerusalem*, which he never read but learned about secondhand. Arendt knew that he was outraged, and she evidently convinced him that at least one of the critics hostile to her was an idiot. What transpired between them on her last visit was, to her mind, an entirely private matter. However, an obituary writer suggested they had a falling out; and for screenwriters with a poetic license, that scene is fair game.

Although Jonas could never agree with Arendt about the responsibility of Jewish leaders for aiding the Holocaust, they did remain friends, even though, according to her biographer Elisabeth Young-Bruehl, they broke off communications for more than a year after he read the Eichmann book. The classroom scene in which Jonas angrily tells her he wants nothing more to do with "Heidegger's favorite student" could have occurred—they both taught at the New School in New York City—but probably did not. In any case, it dramatizes the tension between Arendt's passion for understanding regardless of conventional wisdom and her genius for friendship. Each friend she lost diminished the world, but understanding that world required honest argument between diverse and sometimes divergent opinions.[27]

Drama enlarges our understanding of Arendt. But it is the documentary portion of the film, the archival footage of the Eichmann trial, which supports Arendt's depiction of the accused. It seems as clear as the sight of Eichmann shielded by the glass cage in the courtroom that he shielded himself from reality and factuality by self-deception, lies, and stupidity. We observe a bespectacled, balding man blinking and twisting his lips as he hears testimony. We listen to his bureaucratic explanations: "I received the matter for its immediate processing."

"I can only say that those records were not the authority of Department 4B4." We can only agree with Arendt when, to an Israeli friend, she declares, "Eichmann is no Mephisto."

Yet Eichmann as a character, both in Arendt's book and von Trotta's film, does not reveal the extent to which Eichmann the man was aware of what he did. The German scholar Bettina Stangneth found tapes made in Argentina by a Nazi sympathizer for whom Eichmann played a different role than he did in the trial. Eichmann regrets not having "exterminated the enemy" completely. He boasts that he would have been satisfied to have "killed 10.3 million Jews." He acknowledges being a bureaucrat. "But joined to this cautious bureaucrat was a fanatical fighter for the freedom of the *Blut* [blood] I descend from."[28]

In his essay about Arendt & Eichmann, Mark Lilla argued that she should have written "a book on what she called 'the strange interdependence of thoughtlessness and evil' in modern bureaucratic society" instead of tying her thesis about "the banality of evil" to the story of Eichmann. "No one would have been offended," he said.[29] Yet Arendt's thesis arose from her experience of Eichmann and for her was not entirely separable from it. "I have always believed," she wrote, "that no matter how abstract our theories may sound or how consistent our arguments appear, there are incidents and stories behind them which, at least for ourselves, contain as in a nutshell the full meaning of whatever we have to say."[30] Prior to the Eichmann trial, Arendt had thought in terms of "radical evil." Seeing him in court and reading the interrogation transcripts made her recognize that regardless of the destructive depth of evil deeds, those who do evil may be shockingly shallow. But Eichmann now appears to have been both a fanatic and a functionary, hardly a banal figure.

Lilla's point has the value of exposing a limitation of Arendt's "old-fashioned storytelling" as well as of its cinematic counterpart. Arendt's thesis is widely known because she presented it through a particular story. However, the defendant in a trial, like the protagonist of a play or of a film, can only be a character, without the full complexity of a human being.

Inevitably, then, von Trotta's *Hannah Arendt* does not reveal an important aspect of Hannah Arendt's life and thought. Arendt's reflections about the relationship between thinking, judgment, and morality that the trial engendered ran deeper than her report on Eichmann. Yet even granting the limitations of film as a medium for conveying ideas as well as the complexity of a real person, those reflections could have been dramatized to an extent through the relationship between Arendt and Martin Heidegger.

Heidegger, who served the Nazis in an entirely different and far less consequential capacity than Eichmann, was a profound thinker. The fact that he and Arendt became lovers when she, at eighteen, was his student, has been sensationalized; and she is criticized for honoring him after the war in spite of the fact that Heidegger joined the Nazi party and became rector of Freiburg University during the Third Reich. The film does not fall into the traps of overemphasizing the love affair or of reducing the philosopher to his foolish embrace of Hitler's regime. It shows that Arendt came to Freiburg to study with Heidegger, who, at thirty-five, was a renowned professor, in order to learn how to think. It reveals her shock on seeing a newspaper article about his collaboration with the Nazis. And it portrays her, in a postwar meeting, rebuffing his romantic overtures and suggesting he make a public apology. But that scene misses a point that could have exposed the difference between Arendt's mode of thinking and Heidegger's and that would have shown the influence of the Eichmann trial on themes that preoccupied her subsequently.

When Arendt met Heidegger, rumor had it that "thinking has come to life again; the cultural treasures of the past, believed to be dead, are being made to speak." The screenplay could have had Arendt ask the philosopher why he was so idiotic as to have allied himself with Hitler. What was he thinking? Such a scene would have confronted the audience with a paradox: How was it that Heidegger, who was known for his depth as a thinker, and Eichmann, whose shallowness stemmed from his failure to think, both contributed to, without taking responsibility for, the deeds of the Third Reich?

A clue to the resemblance between the latter's thoughtlessness and the former's profundity appears in *Eichmann in Jerusalem* when Arendt characterizes Eichmann's "inability to think, namely to think from the standpoint of somebody else." Many philosophers, dwelling in their own minds apart from the plurality of everyday life, have lacked that ability. Writing about Heidegger to commemorate his eightieth birthday, Arendt addressed the inadequacy of philosophy to understand politics, a void that she, in her work, strove to fill. "We who wish to honor the thinkers, even if our own residence lies in the middle of the world, can hardly help finding it striking and perhaps exasperating that Plato and Heidegger, when they entered into human affairs, turned to tyrants and führers. This should be imputed not just to the circumstances of the times and even less to preformed character, but rather to what the French call a *déformation professionnelle* [occupational hazard]. For the attraction to the tyrannical can be demonstrated theoretically in many of the great thinkers (Kant is the great exception)."[31]

The ability to think from the standpoint of others and then to make judgments from a frame of reference that goes beyond any one standpoint, including one's own, is an antidote both to the philosophers' abstraction in the realm of ideas and to normal people's thoughtless acquiescence to what everybody around them does and believes in. It is this combination of independent thinking and impartial judging that Arendt applied to her task of understanding the tempests that raged through her times.

She did this in the absence both of a tradition within which to work and of illumination from the public realm. Instead, she found herself in the dark, quoting Bertolt Brecht: "Truly, I live in dark times." What brought that darkness were events of Arendt's lifetime, which included total war, totalitarianism, and genocide. Along with these calamities came the collapse of any credible frame of reference that might have enabled one to interpret them, from religious authority—the death of God that Nietzsche announced—to Hegel's idea, which Marx turned upside down, that world history is the unfolding of Spirit. How could one come to terms with the unpredictable uniqueness of the events that lacerated the twentieth century? Arendt faced the dilemma that Tocqueville described a century earlier: "Since the past has ceased to throw its light onto the future, the mind of man wanders in obscurity."[32]

The one passage in Heidegger's writings that Arendt asked me, as her student, to read contains the sentence, "The light of the public obscures everything" (*"Das Licht der Offenlichkeit verdunkelt alles"*).[33] She said that what ruins everything for him is "the world, that which is public, and the only salvation is the 'self.'" For Heidegger, "the They," or mass mind, spoils the encounter between *Dasein* (being there) and Being that was fundamental to his philosophy. For Arendt, the sentence raised a different issue. She too was concerned about defending the private sphere—that is, the realm of friendship and love—from the mass mind; in privacy one thinks and makes independent judgments. Yet she believed that without people's willingness to enter the public sphere and disclose who they are, there can be no freedom or understanding. This is a venture, she said in an interview, in which "one exposes oneself to the light of the public as a person." To do that requires "a trust in what is human for all people."[34]

Totalitarian rule systematically destroys all places where people may speak and act freely. Yet even in a democracy where we have the ability to express ourselves without fear of censorship or repression, the light of the public obscures quite a lot. Hannah Arendt cast a beacon of clarity through America's darkness. And the way she did it was instructive.

As a teacher and writer, Arendt followed no model of thinking, researching, or reporting. She preferred Lessing's practice of *"Selbst-denken*—independent thinking for oneself,"[35] or, as she liked to put it, "thinking without a bannister." Rather than work within the fields of philosophy, political science, or history, Arendt uniquely blended inquiry, information, analysis, quotations, ideas, and storytelling. It was by crafting narratives incorporating the insights of artists as well as facts and reflections that she sought to understand the subjects that concerned her.

In public as well as in her writings, Arendt came to terms with her times by defining what was new, finding the roots of the new in its antecedents, and refining worn-out words into clear conceptual tools. Her love of poetry animated this activity. Language was her instrument, and in using it, she sought Confucian lucidity through "the rectification of names."

I first saw Arendt on a panel at the Theatre of Ideas in New York City in December 1967. The subject was the legitimacy of violence as a political act, a timely topic in light of the protest over the Vietnam War. She began characteristically by making a distinction: "Power and violence are not the same. Power is inherent in all politics, and all government rests on power. . . . Generally speaking, violence always rises out of impotence. It is the hope of those who have no power to find a substitute for it—and this hope, I think, is in vain. Violence can destroy power, but it can never replace it." That distinction threw light on the war itself as well as on the dispute over how to protest the war, for by rejecting "the common and erroneous equation of power and violence," one perceives "the superiority of the power of the guerrillas [the Vietcong] to an enormous and disastrous display of violence."[36] Having the largest military in the world did not make the United States the most powerful country, as the nation would learn to its sorrow.

Arendt would later say that what the United States sought to achieve through the violence of the war "was neither power nor profit. Nor was it even influence in the world in order to serve particular, tangible interests for the sake of which prestige, an image of the 'greatest power in the world,' was needed and purposefully used. The goal was now the image itself, as is manifest in the very language of the problem-solvers, with their 'scenarios' and 'audiences,' borrowed from the theater."[37] The release of the *Pentagon Papers* by Daniel Ellsberg exposed the fact that the officials in charge of the war knew it could not be won and that they lied systematically to the public. This was a war to maintain credibility at home as the world's most powerful country and to win "minds and hearts" abroad. Complementing and perpetuating violence in Southeast Asia was systematic deception of the public, with the aid of the media, and also of officials, as soldiers reported body counts fabricated to advance careers. Factual truth was the war's first casualty and continual victim, while false stories in lieu of reality were its product and goal. In a situation like this, observed Roger Berkowitz, "when fictional constructions of reality—the very stories and legends that give our world meaning—harden into ideologies and certainties that obscure reality,"[38] Arendt regarded thinking as a political responsibility.

The controversy over the Vietnam War and the ways to oppose it, whether through violent protest, politics, or civil disobedience, gave contemporary relevance to the inquiry Arendt began when she looked at the disaster of the Holocaust face to face. The movie concludes by putting these words on the screen: "The problem of evil became the fundamental subject for Hannah Arendt. She was still struggling with it at the time of her death." Actually, at that time, Arendt was writing a trilogy, *The Life of the Mind*, and she had completed the first two books: *Thinking* and *Willing*. The title page for the third was in her typewriter when she died: *Judging*. The immediate impulse for her "preoccupation with mental activities," she wrote in the introduction, "came from my attending the Eichmann trial in Jerusalem."[39]

In this unfinished work, which Mary McCarthy edited, Arendt examines the experiences at the root of a person's mental powers. What is thinking? How is thinking or the absence of thought related to good judgment on the one hand, and acquiescence in and alliance with evil on the other?

Even though the final Heidegger scene fails to raise these questions, filmmaker Margarethe von Trotta knows well that this was the problem Arendt wrestled with until her last breath. Words appearing briefly on the screen to close out the story of the movie, a reference to "the problem of evil," only suggest the depth of Arendt's post-Eichmann inquiry. But if ever a screenplay had a footnote, it is this one, written by von Trotta and Pam Katz. In an early scene that shows a lively dispute between friends at Arendt and Blücher's apartment in New York City, Arendt says "when the ships are down," and Mary McCarthy corrects her. This is a setup for the climactic scene in which Arendt, explaining what she means by "the banality of evil" to students at the New School, ends her passionate speech with "when the chips are down." That payoff refers to a passage in an essay that anticipates what Arendt might have concluded about thinking and judging had she lived to complete *The Life of the Mind*:

When everybody is swept away unthinkingly by what everybody else does and believes in, those who think are drawn out of hiding because their refusal to join is conspicuous and thereby becomes a kind of action. The purging effect of thinking, Socrates' midwifery, that brings out the implications of unexamined opinions and thereby destroys them— values, doctrines, theories, and even convictions—is political by implication. For this destruction has a liberating effect on another human faculty, the faculty of judgment, which one may call, with some justification, the most political of man's mental abilities. It is the faculty to judge *particulars* without subsuming them under those general rules which can be taught and learned until they grow into habits that can be replaced by other habits and rules. . . .

The manifestation of the wind of thought is no knowledge; it is the ability to tell right from wrong, beautiful from ugly. And this indeed may prevent catastrophes, at least for myself, in the rare moments when the chips are down.[40]

The kind of thinking Arendt described and exemplified, the two-in-one dialogue that enables a person to represent internally the standpoints of others, is a prerequisite for conscience, which preserves the ability to live with oneself. And it makes understanding points of view beyond one's own possible. This ability is crucial for participation in civil society as well as for the art of storytelling.

When an honest exchange of views occurs, minds open up and thinking comes to life. That, for Arendt, was pleasure. "Gladness, not sadness, is talkative," she wrote, "and truly human dialogue differs from mere talk or even discussion in that it is entirely permeated by pleasure in the other person and what he says."[41] A sad consequence of the Eichmann controversy, which made "truly human dialogue" about Hannah Arendt difficult if not impossible for many people over a long period of time, has been a lack of civil discourse especially with regard to the matters that concerned her and that persist in new forms in our time.

Another kind of pleasure comes from the type of judging that Kant described and Arendt had in mind: the esthetic judgment of the spectator. It is a matter of taste: *I* think this is beautiful. *I* think this is wrong. Conventional rules and general standards do not mold the judging of particular things by a liberated mind.

What we judge as spectators are the enduring works and places that constitute the world and also the ephemeral actions that occur between people within the world. It is to remember and understand the human drama that we tell stories. The stories that filmmakers, historians, reporters, and raconteurs tell become subjects for discourse, subject to limitless debate; for, as Arendt wrote, "storytelling reveals meaning without committing the error of defining it."[42] True stories do not provide *the* truth. They do, nonetheless, offer reconciliation with reality and liberation from the shackles of the past; admiration for those who have the courage to exercise their freedom; and stimulus for new stories about what has happened and the way things are.[43]

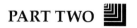

PART TWO

BEGINNINGS AND ENDS

*Experience which is passed on from mouth to mouth is
the source from which all storytellers have drawn.*
—Walter Benjamin

*Every story has a beginning and an end—but
never an absolute end; for the ending of one story
always marks the beginning of another.*
—Ronald Biener

▦ Achilles' Shield

Science and technology progress, but not the arts. "Monuments of unageing intellect,"[1] as Yeats called great works of artistry, are never surpassed. However, new forms of art can break through limits in humanity's visions of the world and create new ways of understanding things.

Dramatic structure along with the key concepts that make documentary storytelling possible originated in the literature of ancient Greece. When fact-based storytelling appeared on stage before citizens of the first democracy, it was a radical innovation. With *The Persians*, Aeschylus did something few playwrights or filmmakers dare to do today: He confronted his public with a sympathetic portrayal of the enemy, in this case the rulers of the Persian Empire that Athenians had defended themselves against, securing their freedom, eight years earlier. The only existing Greek tragedy about living persons and a contemporary event, the play presents King Xerxes, leader of the ill-fated expedition against Greece, and his mother, the Queen, not as enemies or villains but as suffering human beings. "Anxious thoughts now tear apart my heart," says the Queen in her first speech to the chorus. Xerxes, returning home from military catastrophe, asks the chorus—and through the chorus, the audience—to lament with him: "Pluck at your hair and pity the troops." Aeschylus, who fought at Marathon against an army led by Xerxes' father King Darius, a battle in which his brother Cynegeirus was killed, would have the public recognize Persians and Greeks alike as fellow mortals subject to a higher power. "What mortal can escape / God's crafty snare?" asks the chorus. "Man is coaxed in seeming good-will / To the net of ruin / From which he cannot / Escape unscathed."[2]

For Aeschylus, theater was a new art form, and he shaped it decisively, putting actors onstage who speak with each other and not only with the chorus. But impartiality, the practice of looking at an event or subject from various vantage points, including antagonistic points of view, regardless of one's own partiality, is not his innovation. It originated in epic poetry centuries before he was born. A remarkable aspect of *The Iliad* is its full and sympathetic portrayal of Trojans as well as of Greeks. For example, when Hector, the Trojan hero, fights Ajax in single combat and night falls before either prevails, Hector proposes they break off their duel. "Let us make one another memorable gifts," he tells his Greek antagonist, "and afterwards they'll say, among Akhaians / and Trojans: 'These two fought and gave no quarter / in close combat, yet they parted friends.'"[3]

Simone Weil called *The Iliad* the poem of force. That it is. It is unrelenting in its graphic portrayal of the violence of war. But *The Iliad* is also the poem of impartiality. Homer brought impartiality into the world. That breakthrough, both ethical and esthetic, enlarged the scope of human understanding.

Impartiality emerged during the period that Karl Jaspers called the Axial Age and that Karen Armstrong described in *The Great Transformation: The Beginning of our Religious Traditions*. The Axial Age spanned roughly seven centuries from 900 BC to 200 BC. It was a time of rising populations, of large agrarian-based, city-centered empires, of extensive trade routes by caravan and sea, and the spread of alphabetic writing. Jaspers realized that throughout this era, when a great diversity of people encountered each other as never before, "spiritual conflicts arose, accompanied by attempts to convince others through the communications of thoughts, reasons and experiences." This was the period when Buddha, Confucius, Lao Tzu, and the Jewish prophets lived and when ancient Greek civilization grew from Homer to Aeschylus and from Alexander the Great to Archimedes. "In this age," according to Jaspers, "were born the fundamental categories within which we still think today."[4]

After Homer "came Herodotus, who spoke of 'the great deeds of the Greeks *and* the barbarians,'" noted Hannah Arendt. "All of science comes from this spirit, even modern science, and the science of history too." The capacity for impartiality is crucial for democracy as well. In the Athenian *polis*, the original body politic, Arendt wrote, "Greeks learned to *understand*—not to understand one another as individual persons but to look upon the same world from one another's standpoint, to see the same in very different and frequently opposing aspects."[5]

For Arendt, an idea such as impartiality, indeed thought itself, "arises out of the actuality of incident, and incidents of living experience must remain its guideposts by which it takes its bearing if it is not to lose itself."[6] Here is a central purpose for documentary storytelling: keeping alive in the public mind experiences that are the basis for ideas, for science, for democracy, for understanding people very different from oneself.

What, then, is the experience Homer lived through that enabled him to see the world through impartial, even if blind, eyes? The historical record has left no trace of the man or, more likely, men who composed the *The Iliad* and *The Odyssey*. But the epics themselves offer clues to the circumstances that inspired their Olympian vision of human affairs.

Travelers' tales of distant places were a draw in the ancient world, just as letters from the New World were read and discussed in pubs and cafés throughout Europe in the sixteenth century. But travel, as Odysseus's journey shows, was hazardous not only because of storms at sea and other natural dangers. Landing in a new place, a stranger risked his life.

The perils a singer of tales faced as he traveled resound in this episode in *The Odyssey*: Odysseus arrives on the island of Scheria. He does not know how the rulers of the Phaeacians will treat him. Athena protects the hero, obscuring him within a mist as he strides toward the royal palace. When he nears the king and queen, and Athena, rolling back the mist, reveals his presence, Odysseus makes a supplicant's gesture. Flinging his arms around Queen Arete's knees, he begs for mercy and asks for help in getting home. What he has to offer is a tale of hardship, "all I've suffered, thanks to the gods' will." Arete questions him sharply, "Who are you? Where are you from? Who gave you the clothes you're wearing now?" Her underlying question—is he friend or foe? To be perceived as allied or related to a host's enemy is clearly dangerous. "What lands of men have you seen," King Alcinous asks him, "what sturdy towns, what men themselves? Who were wild, savage, lawless? Who were friendly to strangers, god-fearing men?"[7] This is important to know. Odysseus has to find the answers as he travels, often disguising himself and telling lies to conceal his identity. The art of telling a story impartially, to sing the great deeds of the Greeks *and* the barbarians, was the bard's solution—and later, that of the well-traveled "father of history" Herodotus—to the problem of moving through a dangerous world.

Impartiality in itself was not sufficient to create the human world of Homer's epic poems. That required a leap of the imagination that took the mind beyond what Erik H. Erikson called "pseudospeciation"—the tendency to regard those outside one's nationality, clan, or language group as fundamentally Other, beyond the pale, less than human. This tendency is captured in the Greek designation of non-Greeks as barbarians, which means that instead of speaking like human beings, they utter nonsense: bar-bar, bar-bar. Homer's idea that the Olympian gods observe human affairs as *spect*ators gave him a vantage point from which to re*spect* the humanity of all his characters.

These gods are not only observers; they are actors in conflict with each other. The outcome of their disputes among themselves and of their interventions in the lives of mortals generates suspense; one does not know what will happen, which makes for a good story. But the anarchic realm of the gods offers insufficient support for a worldview that includes all mortals. Homer looked beyond the gods to their place for contemplation, Mount Olympus, and beyond the mountains to the cosmos that contains them.

He depicts that cosmos in *The Iliad*, on the shield that the god Hephaistos makes for Achilles. The river ocean streams around the rim, enclosing concentric circles. At the hub, Homer imagines "earth, heaven, and sea, unwearied sun, moon waxing, all the stars." And then, a circle depicting two cities: one at peace with scenes of a wedding feast and of town elders in the marketplace hearing arguments over reparations for a murder; the other city at war, besieged like Troy. In the circle outside that panorama appear ox-plowed fields, a harvest and a vineyard, a bull attacked by lions; and beyond that circle, a dance where "young men and the most desired young girls" move with ease, as when a potter turns her wheel.[8] It is remarkable enough that the art on this shield envisions a cosmos, depicts a form of judgment in settling disputes, and sets war against peace in the images of two cities. Even more striking than the content is its form; for unlike a two- or three-dimensional work of art, the pictures on this imagined shield move in time. Twenty-eight or more centuries before the birth of cinema, the bard of *The Iliad* imagined moving pictures on a symbolic microcosm representing the world.

During the centuries between Homer and Aeschylus, the idea of law evolved in the Greek mind. Solon, who crafted the Athenian constitution, sought justice through the formation of a state ruled by law whose citizens were responsible for its fate.[9] His contemporaries, the Ionian philosophers Thales and Anaximander, laid the foundations of science with the idea of an order that governs nature. What for Homer was the vision of an all-encompassing ocean and what for all Greeks was the perception of a limitless sea became for Thales the doctrine that water is the basic element of the universe. Anaximander realized that Earth is a sphere suspended in space, and he used mathematics to calculate a ratio between Earth's diameter and the lunar cycle around our planet. Thinking nature subject to an immanent rule of law, Thales and Anaximander put their faith in the idea that human reason corresponds to the *logos* of the universe.

Thales, the story goes, fell into a well; and when his maid laughed at him for being so absorbed in the universe he did not look where he

was going, the sage pointed upwards and replied, *"There* is my country."
Thales was the first cosmopolitan, in the largest sense of that word. But
it would take another act of imagination to apply the cosmic concept of
law to the depiction of human affairs here on Earth. No less than from
Dionysian ritual or from its fusion with the Apollonian art of music, as
Nietzsche asserted, Greek tragedy originated with a vision of humanity
subject to a universal law.

Tragic vision, like Homeric impartiality, arose out of harrowing
experience.

When Aeschylus was born, the tyrant Peisistratos ruled Athens.
Having confiscated lands of the aristocratic families from which previous leaders had come, the dictator and his two sons sought popular
support. Their dynasty redistributed land to farmers, administered the
laws fairly, built an aqueduct to supply Athens with water, championed
Athenian athletes in the Olympic games, sponsored works of art and
architecture, instituted recitations of Homer at the Panathenae festival,
and initiated theatrical performances at the festival of Dionysus.[10]

Aeschylus was five or six years old when an aristocratic family drove
the populist tyranny into exile. The upshot was extraordinary. Instead
of the nobility returning to power, Athenians formed a democracy,
establishing equality under the law through a renewed Solonic constitution and creating a legislature run by citizens chosen by lottery.
Every free man had the duty to take part in civic life. Every citizen was
a political actor, responsible in public for his words and deeds. This
new freedom, combined with the ethos of excellence fostered in sports
and the arts by Peisistratos and his sons, inspired loyalty to the *polis*
while encouraging men, regardless of clan or lineage, to realize their
talents fully.[11]

This was the Athens in which Aeschylus grew to manhood. Although
his gravesite tells us only that he was a warrior at Marathon, the poet
probably also took part in the battle of Salamis ten years later, in 480 BC,
when the Athenian fleet annihilated Xerxes' forces. Three hundred war-
ships destroyed an armada of a thousand. A small city-state defeated an
empire. How to account for this astonishing victory, this catastrophic
loss? For Aeschylus, it could only have been a divine power, a god
"who weighing down the balance swung the beam of fortune."[12] This
is the balance of justice, which punishes the hubris of extreme ambition like Xerxes' folly in risking his empire by invading the Greeks. The
outcome put a seal of divine favor on the Athenian democracy in contrast to the empire whose vassal warriors obeyed their master, fearful
of his wrath. Yet Athenians, who like Xerxes enjoyed the freedom to
make decisions and act accordingly, had best be mindful of cosmic law,

however inscrutable it may be. They too might overreach and suffer the consequences. Aeschylus's conviction that "there's a divinity that shapes our ends," as Shakespeare had Hamlet say two thousand years later, inspired the art of tragedy.

In realizing his vision, Aeschylus replaced Olympus, where gods gaze upon the spectacle of human life, with the theater. There, citizens witness scenes of gods and mortals that arouse feelings, inspire awe, and expand awareness.

It was from the cosmic dramas on the ancient Greek stage that concepts used in the craft of documentary storytelling twenty-five centuries later originated. While dramatic form has evolved in various ways and to a great extent in the centuries between the heyday of Athenian democracy and our time, it entails a way of thinking, whether one is drawing from pure imagination, from life, or a combination thereof, that enables the writer to transform a story into a public experience. This way of thinking, known as dramaturgy, is the legacy scriptwriters have in common, whether they write for the stage or the screen, whether their work is fiction or nonfiction.

A key concept that comes directly from tragic drama is character. The concept of character asserts that there are no ordinary people. What everyone has in common is uniqueness. "Character" has to be clearly defined. It is neither the totality of a person's life nor what we call a personality, even though the word "person" comes from *persona*, the mask an actor wore to represent his character in a theatrical performance. Character has consequences. It appears when people remove the personal masks that help them fit in and instead reveal who they uniquely are.

Character is an abstraction similar to the designations of people in the judicial system as witnesses, defendants, and plaintiffs or in the medical system as doctors, nurses, and patients. People bring to the courtroom or to the hospital neither their whole selves nor their general experience; their roles are restricted to what is relevant to the case in question. For the theater or the screen, a writer selects as characters people who have a part to play in relation to the story and represents them in terms of the actions through which the story unfolds. Character is the quality of a person's will. It is revealed through action.

Action, in this context, has to be distinguished from the kind of action often seen in feature films, from car chases to shootouts to the martial arts acrobatics of a so-called "action hero." Nothing of this sort appeared on the ancient stage; battles, murders, and the like occurred offstage. An action may not be spectacular at all. It may consist simply of introducing one person to another. This would be an introduction that has consequences rather than a social nicety, for action also has to be distinguished from behavior. People who behave do what is expected or required of them and of everyone like them in the same situation, while those who act take initiative. Actors "speak what we feel, not what we ought to say," as Edgar says at the close of *King Lear*, a tragedy precipitated by Cordelia's refusal to speak the words that are expected of her, thereby showing her character. A person who acts manifests her will, disclosing who she is in relation to others.[13]

The concepts of character and action guide documentary makers in choosing who to include in their films and which scenes to show. They also influence the storyline: the "arrangement of the incidents" that gives the story unity and keeps people watching. For character is inherently interesting and actions are inherently unpredictable. Whether one says the right thing or blunders, shows courage or cowardice, displays selfishness or generosity under the pressure of a given situation—fighting a battle, responding to disaster, finding money in a stranger's wallet, punishing a child—each choice reveals character. What people are made of becomes clear when the chips are down. Nor can the consequences of any given action be foreseen, since others respond in ways that disclose who they are, taking their own initiatives that influence the outcome. As a result, the playing out of a dramatic story is suspenseful, a quality that holds the interest of the audience. The suspense may have more to do with how things unfold than with what happens. When audience members already know the story that is dramatized, they want to know how a character responds to her fate, not what will occur.

Dramatic form represents that story in the present tense; we experience it as it happens, just as we experience our lives. "It is only a present filled with its own future," as Susanne Langer said, "that is really dramatic."[14] Observing actors at the point of decision, we witness factors and feelings that influence actions they take. The play puts us in their place, but from a distance; and we are no more in the place of the protagonist than that of the antagonist. These words have no moral connotation, the protagonist being simply the one who initiates the action that drives the story, be she Clytemnestra, who resolves to kill her husband, King Agamemnon, when he returns from Troy, or Lysistrata, who proposes to end war by having women withhold sex from their husbands and lovers in protest.

We who observe these characters from our Olympian seats in the theater do so impartially, no matter how heinous the deeds that appear before us. For often what we observe is a reversal of fortune. The workings of the plot may drive a noble character to do evil. Someone who comes onstage as a pariah may, by the end of the play, offer wisdom or a blessing. Theatrical form requires a suspension not only of disbelief but also of judgment. One cannot sense the meaning of the story until it has run its course and all is revealed.

Nor is the meaning explicit. Greek dramas have messengers but no message. Instead, the meaning of the play forms in the minds of the viewers. When a play is profound, that meaning is inexhaustible, to be understood in different ways by different people in different times. "Half of the art of storytelling," as Walter Benjamin wrote, "is to keep a story free from explanation as one reproduces it." This enables one to "interpret things the way he understands them."[15] In the *Agamemnon,* Aeschylus has the chorus invoke "Zeus, who guided men to think / who has laid it down that wisdom / comes alone through suffering."[16] Wisdom, to put it more broadly, "arises out of the actuality of incident."

For dramatists and screenwriters, the practice of impartiality maintains the audience's interest. In the clash between characters, loading the dice robs a play of suspense and moral complexity. Instead, as I. F. Stone realized, "The essence of tragedy is a struggle of right against right."[17] The opposing characters in a play are right in the sense that their actions have validity, stemming from their experience, perspective, and place in the world. So do their feelings, regardless of what they have done. Xerxes' troops killed Greeks, but his pity for the men he commanded elicits sympathy. As audience members, our purpose is to witness and to understand.

That purpose applies even to characters whose actions cannot be considered "right" in any sense: Medea killing her children; bacchantes led by Queen Agave dismembering her son Pentheus; the deranged Ajax slaughtering cattle he mistakes for officers of his own army. Extreme events and great suffering, like that of the wounded and abandoned Philoctetes and of Oedipus, who blinds himself upon realizing he has murdered his father and married his mother, appeared in the Theatre of Dionysus. Aeschylus, Sophocles, and Euripides subjected their audiences to an extraordinary range of experience with plays that evoke passionate feelings and often culminate in the protagonists' recognition that they brought calamity upon themselves. The theatrical viewpoint those dramatists give us combines the distance from which to witness tragic actions with the nearness that allows for empathy.

Their work inspired another form of storytelling that ever since has enabled people to understand actions and events far beyond the limits of their experience. What "history" originally meant was inquiry—to inquire in order to tell how it was, the same word Greeks applied to the protoscientific thinking of the Ionian philosophers. The book that Thucydides, an Athenian general, wrote to tell the story of the Peloponnesian War drew from the art of the tragic poets as it laid the foundations for history as a science. Lacking documentary evidence to represent the facts and memories he had to work with, Thucydides relied on recreations of what people said, as well as narrative descriptions of events. Like a play, *The Peloponnesian War* includes speeches and debates, among them a chilling dialogue between representatives of Athens and the people of Melos, a Spartan colony that Athens had conquered. "My method has been," he wrote, "while keeping as closely as possible to the words that were actually used, to make the speakers say what, in my opinion, was called for in each situation." Thucydides' storyline follows the tragic pattern of Attic theater. The dramatic arc of his plot traces the rise and fall of Alcibiades, the charismatic general who persuaded Athens to launch an ill-fated expedition to Sicily. That attempt to extend the Athenian Empire hastened its decline instead and the loss of the war against Sparta; a story of hubris reminiscent of *The Persians.*

Thucydides' method of inquiry established a precedent not only for the writing of history but also for the making of documentary films. "Different eye-witnesses gave different accounts of the same events, speaking out of partiality for one side or the other or else from imperfect memories," Thucydides wrote. To compensate for bias and error, he "made it a principle not to write down the first story that came my way, and not even to be guided by my own general impressions; either I was present myself at the events which I have described or else I heard of them from eyewitnesses whose reports I have checked with as much thoroughness as possible."[18]

For documentary makers embarking upon a project, the practice of impartiality, inherited from Homer, the tragedians, and Thucydides, enlarges understanding of the subject, whatever their opinions have been. When doing research, it is their responsibility to maintain an open mind as they meet people and interview potential characters. This ability to enter into the minds of a wide range of people characterizes storytellers in every medium. Whether they rely on imagination, as in fiction, or study history, researching lives far removed from their own, or meet and interview strangers, as nonfiction writers do, they go beyond preconceptions and examples drawn from their own limited experience. And when makers give each point of view its best possible representation, they can understand and ultimately show the story from multiple standpoints. "We seldom think about how much freedom it takes to tell even the smallest story," wrote Walter Benjamin. "Any bias robs the narrator of a bit of his articulateness."[19]

The storyteller's quest for understanding is quite different from the Olympian perspective of the gods in that one attains it with a healthy awareness of the limits of one's knowledge and point of view. As Tom Stoppard has Turgenev say in *The Coast of Utopia*, "Putting yourself in another's place is a proper modesty."[20] The process of learning, questioning, and critical thinking that goes beyond personal limits toward a larger vision moves from the bottom up, not the top down.

In documentaries, the virtue of this approach is not only to be fair and to fully understand one's subject but also to be interesting to a larger audience than would watch a biased movie. There is a risk involved. If the makers are intellectually honest, they may create a work that does not conform to what they would like to think or have their viewers believe.

Impartiality may be, as Arendt wrote, "the highest type of objectivity we know,"[21] but it differs significantly from what is considered objectivity in the media. The appearance of objectivity in a documentary mimics the presumed disinterestedness of scientists in their search for knowledge. That can work well in a nature film. But of many subjects, people are not disinterested observers. What impartiality shares with scientific objectivity is the commitment to inquire into what is real and to make that known based on the best available evidence. Yet every maker of documentaries has a range of experience that is both unique and shared with others of the same background and generation; each has opinions and convictions, loyalties and commitments. To pretend that those particularities do not exist by assuming a style of objectivity—the famous "voice of God" of documentary narration—may be a form of dishonesty or self-deception.

Objectivity's claim to a universality that is beyond question reinforces the status quo. Impartiality, in contrast, presents unconventional views and contending representations of reality at their best, thereby raising questions, generating thought, challenging complacent minds and opening avenues for inquiry. While objectivity is deterministic, like a mathematical proof, impartiality requires freedom.

Regarding their subjects, filmmakers need not be impartial. On the contrary, making an independent documentary requires commitment, for success is never certain, and the money raised to complete it is rarely adequate. To make a movie about an architect such as *Places for the Soul* is to want people to know the work of Christopher Alexander. Otherwise, why bother? In *Color Adjustment*, Marlon Riggs proves his point that the changing face of racism has, over the years, influenced the portrayal of black people on television. And in *A Thin Blue Line*, Errol Morris explores the possibility that a juvenile whose testimony led to a man's conviction for murder committed perjury. Film projects often begin with a thesis. When the premise is wrong, the story changes accordingly. Alex Gibney set out to make a film about an American hero until he learned that Lance Armstrong was lying to him and to everyone else. Similarly, scientific experiments put a theory to the test, and trials determine whether the defendant is innocent or guilty as charged. Like scientists, filmmakers have to be impartial with regard to the facts; like judges, they require valid evidence and credible witnesses. Otherwise, their movie may be challenged with good reason, lose its credibility, and fail to achieve its purpose.

Unlike a documentary screenwriter, writers of screenplays for dramatic features need not concern themselves about credibility with respect to anything outside of the worlds they create. They fill the gap between representation and reality with verisimilitude rather than veracity and, in doing so, are more likely to work toward partiality than impartiality.

What feature films do better than any other medium is show the world through the point of view of an individual, literally through that person's eyes. Robert Fulford, writing about the grammar of cinematic narrative that D. W. Griffith invented for *Birth of a Nation*, explains that "a director can guide the audience's point of view, selecting a facial expression here, a tiny corner of the action here. Under his [Griffith's] leadership, films developed as an extension of novels rather than plays." In this way, "movies acquired a mesmeric force never known to the theater."[22] When the opening scene shows a person hit by a car, then cuts to a close-up of her face, we feel her pain. When an attractive man meets an attractive woman, we want them to make love, to survive, to succeed in spite of the obstacles they face. Immersed in a chase or a prison escape, we have what Sartre called "a carnal relationship with an image, not merely knowledge of it."[23]

According to screenwriting guru Robert McKee, "The classically told story usually places a single protagonist—man, woman, or child—at the heart of the telling."[24] He claims that a film that follows this classical design "is a mirror of the human mind." By "the human mind," McKee of course means one person's viewpoint. Cosmologist Lisa Randall has a larger view: "Our limited perspective makes us forget that the human experience is a vast locus of points of which we are but one." Randall calls for "a deliberate and consistent effort to step out of our familiar frames of reference. Only then can we synthesize different perspectives, observations, and experience—the very act at the heart of creativity, which will be essential to solving the increasingly complex problems that beset our world."[25] Documentaries respond to this challenge.

Some documentary filmmakers do use the medium's ability to foster identification with a single person. This is especially the case when they appear in their own movies: Deanne Borshay Liem, who was adopted by a California family, goes to Korea in search of her birth mother, in *First Person Plural*; Deborah Hoffmann visits her mother through the camera eye, in *Complaints of a Dutiful Daughter*, and her mother, who has Alzheimer's, cannot recognize her; Justine Shapiro takes Mateo, her six-year-old son, to meet Persians and make friends in *Our Summer in Tehran*—manifesting their mutual humanity during an era when the United States and Israel are threatening to bomb Iran. These directors use the power of their presence to bring the viewer beyond fantasies and familiar experiences. They have no script; they do not know in advance what will happen. Film editor Walter Murch puts it this way: "In regular movies, the director is God. In a documentary, God is the director."

From his first movie on, the onscreen provocateur Michael Moore cast himself as a working class hero with a chip on his shoulder. In doing so, Moore demonstrates that a documentary's entertainment value can make it popular and profitable. The pleasure he offers comes in part from seeing others react to him. Scenes in which Moore demands an interview with Roger Smith at General Motors or confronts Charlton Heston for holding a National Rifle Association meeting in Colorado soon after a high-school massacre in that state have dramatic tension that comes from no one knowing what will happen. Moore's films have educational as well as entertainment value, for the film-maker raises questions and searches for knowledge in the course of his adventures. He does "synthesize different perspectives, observations, and experience." Although Moore is known for his politics, he says, "the art of the movie is more important to [him] than the politics."[26] Indeed, what he learns from practicing his art gives him a depth and breadth of knowledge that undermines conventional wisdom. In 2016, Moore stood out among the myriad of political thinkers by predicting and understanding the victory of Donald Trump.

The roles that Deanne Borshay Liem, Deborah Hoffman, Justine Shapiro, Michael Moore, Morgan Spurlock, Yoav Shamir, Ai Weiwei, and other onscreen directors play as protagonists in their own films show the openness of nonfiction filmmaking to innovation. There are no rules independent filmmakers have to follow. Some documentaries stage dramatizations just as some narrative features use archival footage and documentary camera techniques. The mutual influence of fiction and nonfiction films is an ongoing experiment, much like the influence dramatic form has had on movies and movies on theater for more than a century. At the end of the day, the public decides what is worth watching. To reach that public, a documentary has to represent the actual world in a credible way. For while documentaries can be entertaining as well as enlightening and educational, credible representation is what spectators, beset by deceptive ads, overabundant information, political mendacity, and superficial if not distorted news, expect and depend on. Such representation requires taking into account a multiplicity of perspectives. And the dramatic form that governs films that do this draws from ancient, enduring innovations in the artistic portrayal of reality.

⊞ FIRE IN THE CAVE

Cinema emerged from the fusion of a chemical process, photography, and a form of energy, electricity, which, moving photographic images through a projector onto a lighted screen, generates an illusion of experience. This breakthrough was not the first of its kind. The combination of images drawn with a variety of mineral pigments and an innovative use of fire to illuminate cave walls brought images of animals and stories told about them compellingly to life.

Realistic portraits of bears, horses, stags, bison, rhinos, and lions animate the chambers within the 800-foot-long Chauvet Cave in southern France. For those who created and witnessed this astonishing art, flames fought the darkness. Charcoal on the cave floor attests to fires kindled tens of thousands of years ago. Remnants of a grease lamp, whose plant-stem wick extended from a lump of fat held in a hollow stone, show how artists lit the walls they painted on.[1]

Several tableaus represent animals in motion. Horse heads, one atop the other, suggest a running herd. A pride of lions, facing in one direction, seems to advance. Rhinos appear side by side, some with multiple horns, as if shaking their heads up and down. "The desire to make images move, the need to capture movement," wrote Martin Scorsese, "seemed to be with us 30,000 years ago in the cave paintings at Chauvet—in one image a bison appears to have multiple sets of legs, and perhaps that was the artist's way of creating the impression of movement."[2] Unlike Eadweard Muybridge's sequential photos of a trotting horse, an experiment that set the stage for the motion picture, these images could only be a dream, rather than a forerunner, of the movies. Still, for those looking at them in flickering firelight, the sense of animals moving across the cave walls must have felt amazingly real.

There is no evidence that people lived inside this cave, no remains of cooked bones. This was a ceremonial place. Long ago, upon a pedestal of stone, someone placed the skull of a bear. One imagines Chauvet to have been a sacred site where artist/shamans summoned animal spirits, where celebrants by firelight told stories, sang and danced, strengthened their fellowship, raised courage for the hunt. Using specially designed battery-powered lights, Werner Herzog filmed this *Cave of Forgotten Dreams*. His 3D movie is a tribute to the ancestors of every artist and every filmmaker.

"Human beings are actors in a story," wrote the naturalist E. O. Wilson. "We are the growing point of an unfinished epic."[3] Measured on a timeline marking the tens of millennia of creative representations of actuality, the kinds of fire that move photos, run videocams, and process data are extremely new. Not only does electricity propel media, it enables people to live continually within manufactured structures where they rely on strangers' accounts of reality. The enclosures that electrification plus architecture plus mass media built, beginning in the twentieth century, can snare their inhabitants like Plato's cave, whose denizens watch firelit shadow plays unaware of the world beneath the Sun. Wittgenstein warned of the "bewitchment of our intelligence by means of language."[4] Even more seductive is the bewitchment that cinematic sights and recorded sounds interpreted by language makes possible. Mass media inform, entertain, educate, and opinionate; they pump the economic bloodstream and swell the arteries of the body politic. But when marginalized groups seek exposure in the public sphere, when crises occur for which there are no ready-made explanations, when dangers loom that the powerful won't acknowledge, having independent ways of looking at things matters greatly.

Independently produced documentaries that address subjects that are both controversial and consequential rarely make an appearance in public without a struggle. One communications scholar describes this struggle as "a shadow play of mythology." According to B. J. Bullert, "Independent producers, public television gatekeepers, journalists, reviewers, and members of interest groups are soldiers battling on a field of myths and beliefs—battling to maintain or resist prevailing ideologies that serve established, powerful interests that underpin our social, economic, and political order."[5]

Nuclear fission and fusion are new kinds of fire under the Sun, and the shadows they cast fall everywhere. Many independent filmmakers were launching their careers, thanks to the availability of affordable filmmaking technologies, when a critically dangerous phase of the Cold War put countless lives, and places that harbor life, at risk.

In the late 1970s and early '80s, the use of nuclear and thermonuclear weapons not only for testing and the intimidation of adversaries but also for bombing, for the first time since Hiroshima and Nagasaki, seemed imminent. As during the Cuban Missile Crisis in the sixties, the placement of nuclear weapons, this time Pershing II and cruise missiles in Europe, threatened to provoke, rather than defend against, nuclear war. Also during this period, the partial meltdown of a nuclear reactor at Three Mile Island raised fears that nuclear power plants were too dangerous to be tolerated. That was "the event that galvanized me into involvement with the nuclear issue," recalled David L. Brown. "I immediately shelved my project on the zen of sport that I'd been shooting for over a year to focus on the nuclear power issue."[6] Brown spent the next fourteen years making films about nuclear power, nuclear weapons, and the antinuclear movement, culminating with *Bound by the Wind*, which chronicles nuclear weapons tests in the atmosphere and the global campaign that succeeded in banning them.

Brown and other nonfiction filmmakers sought to provide perspective to dispel perplexity, knowledge to replace ignorance and propaganda, and tales of courage to overcome fear. Among the hundreds of independently produced documentaries they made are *The Day After Trinity: J. Robert Oppenheimer and the Atomic Bomb* (1980) by Jon Else; *The Atomic Café* (1982) by Archives Project members, including Kevin and Pierce Rafferty and Jayne Loader; and *Dark Circle* (1982) by Chris Beaver, Judy Irving, and Ruth Landy.

The makers of *Dark Circle* are members of the community of independent media professionals that I joined after returning to San Francisco from Humboldt County in 1980. I had been writing for a theater group, the Dell'Arte Players Company, whose first production, *Loon's Rage*, dramatized a meltdown in a nuclear power plant, farcically anticipating the Three Mile Island disaster.[7] Soon after moving back to the Bay Area, I became interested in and impressed by the filmmakers' work-in-progress about nuclear technology.

It took Beaver, Irving, and Landy five years to complete *Dark Circle*. That was due not only to the vagaries of fundraising but also to difficulties inherent in their subject and to their determination to develop an effective dramatic form for the content they chose.

They focused on plutonium, a subject enshrouded at that time in many layers of government secrecy. It took extensive archival research and diligent use of the Freedom of Information Act to uncover the footage and information they needed. They learned, for example, that plutonium-239, an isotope used to generate nuclear chain reactions in bombs and power plants, has a half-life of more than 24,000 years, about three-quarters of the timespan between themselves and the artists of Chauvet. Lacking a unifying story, they decided to weave together "atomic biographies" in search of a storyline. The filmmakers had a clear purpose: to bring to public attention the lives of people who are affected by plutonium, whether in the form of a bomb, a power plant, or a production facility. Going forth with a camera, they shot almost everything and everyone they could find that had something to do with plutonium.

There were some givens. Historically, the A-bomb that destroyed Nagasaki was made of plutonium. And geographically, the filmmakers had a starting point: Rocky Flats, near Denver, Colorado. Plutonium "buttons," small A-bombs in themselves, were manufactured there as triggers for H-bombs—thermonuclear weapons. But there were other aspects of the subject that somehow had to enter into the picture: the nuclear arms race; the effects of nuclear explosions and radioactive contamination on human health; the fact that nuclear reactors, like the one then being built at Diablo Canyon in California, generate plutonium; and the campaign against nuclear power.

During the course of editing, through years of trial and error, the filmmakers learned which stories best dramatized their concerns. They decided which scenes to include and where to place them: the "arrangement of the incidents," as Aristotle put it. They had to remove one compelling story: that of Karen Silkwood, a whistleblowing worker in the Kerr McGee plutonium production plant who died in a mysterious car crash en route to meeting a *New York Times* reporter. That episode required a film of its own. They divided the content into acts—introducing their subject, developing their stories, and coming to a conclusion. In itself, their subject had no inherent beginning and ending; these had to be crafted. They found ways to connect, via transitions, the various storylines. And they figured out how to win viewers' interest in their subject despite the resistance many people felt, then as now, to knowing about it.[8]

Plutonium unleashes on Earth the force that fuels the stars. A film about plutonium offers none of the pleasures of the horror movie, whose figure of doom is readily visible and ultimately, after turns of the plot, conquerable. Telling its story challenges those who believe that plutonium is a matter best left to the experts: people qualified to understand it and capable, one likes to feel, of keeping it under control.

No expert can star in such a movie; no hero can save the day. A technology triggered by something unimaginably minuscule that wreaks destruction on an enormous scale and scatters highly toxic contaminants that last millennia is so incredible that those who tell its story, especially if they lack professional authority as experts, have a daunting task.

The first thing a documentary has to do, no matter how difficult its subject, is seize the spectators' attention. "Attention," noted neuroscientist Christof Koch, "is evolution's answer to information overload;

it is a consequence of the fact that no brain can process all available information."[9] Looking at a lighted screen in a dark room or theater sets the expectation famously expressed by Yogi Berra: "You can observe a lot just by watching." From that point the movie does what, according to Koch, attention does: "selective processing of images." Consider driving a car or playing a game: for a motion picture to replace that process in viewers' minds, what they have to do is "just watch." What the show must do is hold their attention.

At the beginning and end of the film, *Dark Circle* displays two visually beautiful, thought-provoking sights, revealing time and space from a planetary perspective.

One is the migration of geese between Mexico and Canada. Shifting in formation as one purposeful organism, the flock becomes a symbol of the continuity of life on Earth. As we see them fly, the narrator, Judy Irving, tells us that four billion years ago, life appeared on Earth; one million years ago, geese began to migrate; five thousand years ago, people started to record history; and decades ago, the birth of the nuclear age threatened to block the pathway—that passage through the sky of time—of evolution.

The other iconic image in *Dark Circle* is a total solar eclipse. During this rare, dramatic event, the Earth is a stage, with its moon coming between the planet and the Sun. What we will witness in the film is of global concern, that symbol suggests. A total eclipse implies that the blackness is temporary: the eclipse will pass, the Sun's warmth and illumination will return. The form of the circle, dark though it is, reassures. But it also warns. A clip from a film produced by National Educational Television in 1963 shows workers in lab coats who manipulate pieces of plutonium using gloves thrust into sealed chambers. Standing beside them, a scientist informs us that in a lifetime, a human being can tolerate less than a millionth of a gram. The reporter interviewing him concludes that plutonium, once released into the environment, "may come back to you." That too is a dark circle.

Having won viewers' attention, the film now has to tell its story clearly and credibly without arousing apocalyptic fears or escapist hopes—common responses in that time when the superpowers in their rivalry relied on a "balance of terror."

As a form of communication, documentaries are well suited to let new ways of looking at things unfold. Often an unseen character, the voice-over narrator, offers a bridge between the viewer and the world of the film. Unlike feature films that forge audience identification with a protagonist or a set of characters, documentaries typically maintain some distance between the public and the people onscreen. Yet like feature films, documentaries have to engage the audience, a task that can be difficult for an unembodied voice. One solution to this problem is to show the narrator at the outset of the film. The eloquence of the narration and the authenticity of the narrator can engage the audience whether she is seen or not. But the most powerful approach is to make an existential connection with whoever is watching the show. This may occur through images, as when, in a film about a disease, one sees in rapid succession before-and-after pictures—healthy now, ravaged later—and realizes, this could happen to me.

Dark Circle uses all of these techniques.

What is striking is the simplicity of the story that narrator/filmmaker Irving tells early in Act One; it is a story everyone can relate to. Irving was in Denver when she saw a magazine article reporting that plutonium from the Rocky Flats Nuclear Weapons Facility, sixteen miles northeast of the city, was contaminating its water supply. Suddenly, she wondered whether a glass of water she drank would give her cancer.

Judy Irving does not speak on camera. But early on, we see a photo of her as a child. Irving tells us that she learned to "duck and cover" in the event of nuclear war, to believe in "Atoms for Peace," and to rely on "our friend, the atom."

The film soon takes us to Rocky Flats where we meet Don Gable, a thirty-three-year-old worker who is dying of brain cancer. He was exposed to a release of plutonium at the plant; a pipe near his head leaked. Gable is bald, his face is bloated, his skull indented on one side. He speaks with difficulty. We see a photo of Gable six months earlier: a handsome man with dark hair. Six months after the interview, he is dead.

This evidence of plutonium's fatal reach, like the knowledge, as Samuel Johnson told Boswell, that one will soon be hanged, "concentrates the mind wonderfully." Now, despite the dread many feel of facing the subjects of nuclear destruction and radioactive contamination, the audience is hooked. We need to know more about this deadly element.

Yet an effective introduction to the subject does not ensure a coherent treatment. Like a drama, a film requires what Aristotle called "unity of action." In this case, the unity is both external and internal. What holds the film together overall is the filmmakers' quest, motivated by the potentially lethal drink of water, to explore what plutonium is; why, where, and how it is produced; what it has done to the world; and what people are doing about it. This quest is personal only at the start: Irving's narration soon shifts from first to third person. If the subject were not so variegated, if it had a natural storyline, sheer report-age could carry the viewer through. But this film required a central, internal story, not to connect the dots—narration does that—but rather to make us realize what it means to live in the shadow of plutonium and, given this onerous situation, to pose a dilemma that needs resolution, creating suspense that keeps people watching to the end.

Dark Circle's unifying drama is the story of Marlene Batley. The mother of two girls, she lives a few miles from Rocky Flats. She stands in front of a large mound of rocks and dirt near her house where happy children, hers and neighbors', play. When the Batleys bought that house, she tells us, they were not informed there was a nuclear weapons plant nearby. The salesman said that the Federal Housing Authority would not guarantee their loan because of a problem with the soil sample. Asked what the problem was, he claimed there might be a water table under the land. Later, Batley learned that the soil was contaminated with plutonium. She worries about minute particles of dust in her house and the milk the children drink. She seems distressed as she looks back at her girls playing on the dirt pile.

This is anecdotal—a mother's fears. But *Dark Circle* soon substantiates what she says. The visual transition from that scene is misleading: the sight of cows grazing near Rocky Flats. The filmmakers did not know that these were beef, not dairy cows. But the narrator's reference to a soil analysis in 1954 by Dr. Carl Johnson, the county health director and a professor of preventive medicine, puts Batley's fears on firm ground. Two years after Rocky Flats began operations, Johnson found 285 times more plutonium than the Department of Energy claimed it detected on land slated for the housing developments near Rocky Flats. In 1957, Irving informs us, a major plutonium fire at the plant sent clouds of plutonium oxide over Denver (an episode reported in the *New York Times* in 1981). After another fire, in 1969, that released more radio-active materials into the countryside, we see Brigadier General Edward Giller of the Atomic Energy Commission claim that a negligible quantity of plutonium oxide escaped due to the fire: "It amounts to a very small fraction of what the plant has released in the normal operating procedures that have been there." Does Batley have reason to fear for her family's health? That is for the viewer to decide.

More evidence of the toxic effects of plutonium comes from a nearby farm. Lloyd Mixon describes newborn pigs with mouths too malformed to nurse, feet too twisted to walk, internal organs grown outside their bodies. He recalls chicks hatched with their brains atop their heads and others stillborn in the shell, their weirdly shaped beaks incapable of breaking through. He himself had several cancerous tumors surgically removed. Plutonium was found in his tissues and in some of the mutated animals on his land.

Rex Haag, a house builder who lives, like the Batleys, three miles from Rocky Flats, mourns his daughter, Kris. She died at age twelve of cancer. A lab analysis of her ashes found a large amount of plutonium. Immediately after seeing this story, we meet Dr. Marilyn Werkema of the Rocky Flats staff. She asks local residents to keep an open mind. Health effects from the plant, she says, "are estimated to be too small to measure." After a horse rancher argues that the EPA health safety standards were not established by medical personnel but rather by former Atomic Energy Commission staff, Werkema replies, "I believe Rocky Flats is a safe, healthful place, and the environment around it likewise is safe and a healthful place to live."

As communication scholar B. J. Bullert noted, writing about *Dark Circle* in her book on the politics of public television, "The film makers portrayed the officials as players in a drama rather than authorities who somehow stand outside it."[10] Those speaking for the nuclear industry stand on the same stage as the residents. The pained expression on Dr. Werkema's face does not inspire confidence.

Irving tells us that the woman who organized this meeting "found 23 cancer cases among her immediate neighbors" and that Don Gable knew two women who lived near him who, like him, were dying of brain cancer. We meet them. Bea Campbell, wearing a curly wig, admits she doesn't know anything about Rocky Flats, and it seems farfetched that the nuclear weapons plant could be the cause of her cancer, "but not any more farfetched than us in the same area get the same thing."

Now, in Act Two, we see Marlene Batley once again. Walking door-to-door with her daughters, Batley asks her neighbors if they have any concerns about the nearby production of plutonium. This sequence follows the "rule of three." The first neighbor, a woman seen through a screen door, says, "It doesn't bother me. I knew about it before I bought the house." The second neighbor, a man sitting on his front deck, tells Batley, "I'm not concerned." The third, a woman, says, "I've wanted to get in touch with you."

The rule of three applies to everything from works of art to jokes. While one and two are only this and that, three can imply a number beyond itself. When two circles with the same radius intersect and when the center of each circle touches the other's perimeter, a third form appears: the almond-shaped mandorla. This is found in Venn diagrams and many religious paintings. The desired result is an opening of minds: the suggestion, representation, or invocation of what lies beyond the immediate this and that. It is the door that, we suppose,

Batley walks through after she meets the third neighbor. The rule of three as applied to Batley's visits to nearby houses follows a setup, elaboration, and payoff progression. This, on a small scale, reflects the three-act structure of the film as a whole.

Marlene Batley's activism precedes sequences in the film that show a demonstration to build opposition to Rocky Flats and a civil disobedience campaign to blockade construction and prevent completion of the Diablo Canyon nuclear power plant on the coast of southern California. A woman whose husband works at Rocky Flats speaks at a rally opposing nuclear weaponry in spite of her fear that he will lose his job.

Then we hear an argument for nuclear weapons by a physicist who designs them. "Nuclear weapons are a horror to the future existence of civilization," says Stirling Colgate. "They've made the ante for war so high that it is almost a decision of mutual assured suicide for the world to be involved with a nuclear war. And the only way I know to preserve our culture is to make sure that we continually have the ante in response of nuclear weapons as high as you need to make the other, whoever is the aggressor, feel that there is no way that they can find an advantage by attacking and dominating you." This is the official rationale for the nuclear arms race between the superpowers, the narrator points out. Regardless of our politics, whatever our sympathies, we encounter Colgate personally, at home in front of his fireplace, not just as an expert. He describes himself as "a male human being that likes to see explosions." The film not only draws out his best argument for the product of Rocky Flats, it shows his humanity.

Dark Circle could have landed squarely on one side of the nuclear/antinuclear polarity that it dramatizes. But the filmmakers sought knowledge and understanding, not political points and moral certainty. In our final encounter with Marlene Batley, in Act Three, the mother we sympathize with, whose fears for her family resonate with ours, has undergone a twist of fate. The Batleys are moving. They don't want prospective buyers to know about Rocky Flats; that "could cost the sale of my house." And they don't want a young family to buy the house. "As I watched Marlene make her final decisions," says Judy Irving, "I asked myself what I would have done." Marlene and Woody did sell to a couple with two children, like themselves. They had come full circle.

Dark Circle does not judge them. The film does not take sides where Marlene Batley is concerned; it does not tell viewers what to think about the choice she must make. Rather it has them put themselves in her place. This is what Hannah Arendt called "situated impartiality." To understand people who are different in kind or have different interests or who are distant in time and place from oneself, "one trains one's imagination to go visiting," to take "the viewpoints of others into account."[11]

The moral complexity of the Batleys' situation reflects the difficulty on all scales, from the individual to the nation to the world, of extrication from the nuclear threat. The need for jobs, for energy, and for security all weigh in the balance, making it convenient to rationalize the situation, to postpone the day of reckoning, to ignore the dilemma altogether. To obtain a larger view, wrote Arendt, one has to look beyond "what we usually call self-interest, which, according to Kant, is not enlightened or capable of enlightenment but is in fact limiting." By "visiting" the widest range of viewpoints concerned with the issue in question, a filmmaker arrives at a place from which the public may consider the matter sympathetically, but also critically, and form enlightened judgments.

The film ends with two encouraging sequences. Nancy Woods, the woman who spoke out against Rocky Flats although her husband worked there, announces at a demonstration that he quit his job and opened a small business. He uses "his machine skills for something besides making bombs," she tells a reporter. Civil disobedience at the gates of Diablo Canyon, the nuclear plant built directly on an earthquake fault near San Luis Obispo, delays its opening after the license for operation is approved. Then, a twenty-five-year-old engineer finds that blueprints for the two mirror-image reactors have been mixed up. Earthquake supports for the cooling pipes that would prevent a meltdown were installed backwards. As a result, the license is suspended. The engineer claims that the nonviolent blockade did not influence him. Be that as it may, the demonstrators, hundreds of whom were arrested and jailed, bought time for his discovery.

This turn in the plot that brings an unexpected last-minute victory to the demonstrators dramatizes the theme that rather than rely on the expertise of nuclear industry professionals, let us heed the experiences of everyday people who are affected by this technology. In dramatic form, it is the outcome of the plot that yields the story's meaning. This meaning is not explicit; it's not a message. Instead of being told what to think, viewers are encouraged *to* think. That is the mandorla the third act opens up. That is the light that follows the darkness of totality.

As we see solar rays emerging from the eclipse, the narrator concludes that although we have not suffered a nuclear war, our own nuclear weapons have begun "to kill us, not only in the body but in the spirit as well. It may not be the experts who finally break this dark circle," she says. "It may not be the experts who lead us out of the Atomic Age and into the next." With sunlight returning to the world, brant geese weave intricately shifting patterns through the sky. Then the credits roll.

○

Beginning with its premiere at the New York Film Festival in 1982, *Dark Circle* won critical acclaim. It received a national Emmy Award for "outstanding achievement in news and documentary," a "Certificate of Special Merit" from the Academy of Motion Picture Arts and Sciences, and the Grand Prize for documentary at the Sundance Film Festival. Getting the film on public television, however, proved to be a struggle. The conflict that ensued exposed a chasm. One side Bullert characterized as "the preferred PBS style of public affairs documentaries with dispassionate narrators, certified talking head experts from opposing camps, and little or no music." On the other side: "the feature-documentary tradition in the United States."

The players in this drama were the makers of *Dark Circle* and executives both at national PBS and at KQED, the San Francisco affiliate. What Bullert described as "a shadow play" can be divided into acts and scenes culminating with an unexpected twist that brings about the denouement.

To raise the curtain, the producers, our protagonists, sent a videotape to Pam Porter, who was in charge of acquisitions for KQED. In August 1984, Porter sent the program to Barry Chase, vice president of news and public affairs for PBS. She informed him that KQED agreed to be the film's "presenting station"—its launchpad for national broadcast. In April 1985, Chase's subordinate, Gail Christian, told the filmmakers that *Dark Circle* would be broadcast at 10:00 PM on a weeknight on PBS. In August, Porter notified Christian that the filmmakers had raised the funds required for publicity and other expenses related to the broadcast. She asked the PBS executive for an airdate.

After this exposition came dramatic conflict. KQED's current affairs director Beverly Ornstein believed that *Dark Circle* was not a work of journalism the station could stand behind. She complained that the film "should have gone to the current affairs department rather than the acquisitions department because then it wouldn't have gotten to PBS." Ornstein told Nat Katzman, manager and vice president of KQED, that *Dark Circle* lacked "sufficient documentary evidence to substantiate the conclusion alleged on the screen. The heavy-handed editorializing in the way it was edited contributed to the feeling that the documentary was driven by point of view rather than by documentary evidence and facts." Katzman did not think "the claims in the show were false." But he doubted the credibility of Irving, Beaver, and Landy; he had "the uncomfortable feeling that this is propaganda, not journalism." As a consequence, KQED decided not to put its "presenting station" logo on *Dark Circle* after all.

Alarmed by this reversal, Barry Chase and his associates at PBS voted to rescind Gail Christian's decision to broadcast the film. Christian, a former news director, objected. She thought the film was well researched. "It was almost an unwillingness on the part of PBS staff to believe that the Rocky Flats plant had poisoned the entire community around it," Christian recalled. "They were not going to believe that this is the way we do business in America, and that meant the film makers obviously had to be wrong."

These arguments went on without the makers' knowledge. Not only had they raised thousands of dollars to cover "step-up costs" for the broadcast, they filmed an introduction by Colorado Representative Pat Schroeder. All they heard from Pam Porter, their point of contact, was that PBS had questions for them to answer before scheduling the program. When the list of questions did not come, Chris Beaver called Gail Christian. The questions PBS had "are crazy," Christian said. The panel of "six little quakey, shaky people in a room" wanted the filmmakers to verify the distance between Rocky Flats and Denver, the time it took for the black brant to migrate between Alaska and Mexico, and scores of other details. "It's the goddamn system," she told Beaver. "If KQED would put their logo on, I could give you an airdate within weeks."

KQED's refusal to present the program was not the issue according to Beverly Ornstein. PBS could broadcast the show on their own at any time. "Chase had the same concerns about the journalism that we did, so he didn't want to do it."

Unwilling to give up, Gail Christian tried to find a compromise that would persuade Chase to go ahead with the broadcast. The ideas included adding a panel discussion after the show, adding a disclaimer saying that the show promoted "a particular point of view," and having the program reedited. One sequence in particular was on the chopping block. It shows a weapons convention where corporations sell products to the US military. This military–industrial gathering ushers in a display of logos of participants in making nuclear weapons. In this context, their slogans are disturbingly ironic: GE—"We bring good things to life"; Union Carbide—"Today, something we do will touch your life"; the University of California—"Let there be light." The filmmakers refused to cut it.

Everyone was in the dark. Not knowing that the broadcast was in jeopardy, Beaver, Irving, and Landy proceeded to purchase mailing lists and develop publicity materials. Nat Katzman of KQED, who wanted to get the show on the air despite his doubts about the filmmakers, did not understand PBS's rejection of the broadcast. Gail Christian had no idea of what compromise the filmmakers would agree to that PBS would accept. Finally, she asked KQED to produce a half-hour debate following the show that would balance its point of view. Furious, the filmmakers rejected that proposal and made the controversy public.

Were this shadow play a film or stage play, Act Two would begin here. Often a change of scene, the entrance of a new and significant character, or an expansion of the frame of reference marks the transition from exposition and initial conflict to the development of the story. In *Dark Circle*, all of these occur. The flight of geese takes us to a new place and to a new actor, a *re*actor where plutonium, along with other radioactive waste, is born: Diablo Canyon. In the drama of the controversy over broadcasting this film, PBS's refusal to screen it uncut and without a panel or debate to "balance" it became toxic. The filmmakers protested publicly and threatened to sue. Chase accused them of bias. "The film's structure and narrative leave no question about where the producers stand," he wrote Katzman. However, Chase later told Bullert that he refused to broadcast a program that addressed national security issues because he had not trusted the filmmakers. They were, he admitted, "ahead of their time with the story."

Breaking an important story before anyone else is of course the goal of any news organization. As for the accusation that the film is biased—the same can be said of those who dismissed the evidence that plutonium production at Rocky Flats exposed workers to radiation and contaminated the surrounding land, causing cancer and birth defects among people and animals in its vicinity. The "balance" to what *Dark Circle* reveals would have come from people who were willing to accept and conceal the death of citizens as the price of producing nuclear weapons; it would have come from people willing to risk the death of millions in the event of nuclear war. To be impartial does not mean to be insensate. To call biased those who favor health over disease, peace over war, and life over death is to prefer madness to sanity.

The shadow play had a third act. Executive producer Marc Weiss, a friend of the producers of *Dark Circle*, opened up a strand of PBS programming dedicated to the work of independent documentary film-makers. He founded the series POV with the *Dark Circle* controversy in mind. But by August 1989, when PBS broadcast the film on POV, its exposé of Rocky Flats was no longer news. In June, agents from the EPA and the FBI had raided the nuclear weapons plant to collect evidence of its violations of federal environmental laws. In 1992, Rocky Flats was closed after operators of the facility pled guilty to criminal charges, fully vindicating the filmmakers' assertion that they based their work on accurate information.

One irony of the *Dark Circle* saga is that this model of impartial independent filmmaking became the poster child for POV. When a documentary dares to present aspects of the world that do not fall within acceptable boundaries, gatekeepers of public opinion dismiss it as merely a point of view. For *Dark Circle* to be broadcast under the POV umbrella suggests that the perspective it offers is first-person singular rather than a valid multifaceted view of the way things are. Bullert defines the feature-documentary tradition as "a genre that encourages films with strong points of view, the use of innovative and dramatic techniques, and a willingness to address divisive issues that have not been sanctioned by the *New York Times.*" Yes, there are strong points of view in *Dark Circle,* but to my mind, the film transcends them all. With its open-minded narration and insistence on giving contending opinions a fair hearing, *Dark Circle* exemplifies the search for reality via the exploration of its subject as seen through a multiplicity of perspectives and supported by thorough research.[12] To call *Dark Circle* a POV film is to marginalize it while concealing the falsehood of the official media's claim to unbiased comprehensiveness.

Some documentaries do express *a* point of view, showing stories through the prism of an individual's subjectivity. This one provides something greater: what Kant called an "enlarged mentality." Its vision of reality is as different from the personally subjective nonfiction film as it is from the presentation of opposing views within a narrow band of opinion that passes for news analysis on PBS. The appearance of neutrality, like the presumption of objectivity, must not be confused with impartiality. Instead, it expresses a mindset that serves the status quo by producing content that does not ruffle complacent states of mind. The independent documentary, in contrast, uncovers what lies beneath the "coverage."

Another way to make this distinction is to emphasize the need news programs have for a consistent format. Lacking the time to tailor each presentation to its subject, they rely on formulas. The Viennese satirist Karl Kraus's contrast between two kinds of writers, "those who are and those who aren't," applies to this difference between independent documentaries and mainstream news programs. "With the first, content and form belong together like soul and body; with the second, content and form fit together like body and clothing."[13] In news programs, one size fits all. Independent filmmakers find the soul of their subject.

⊞ THEATER OF HISTORY

Tens of thousands of years ago, the discovery of sailing accelerated humanity's great migration, as did the domestication of horses beginning about six thousand years ago. But it wasn't until the Industrial Revolution produced fossil fuel–burning machines that people managed to travel thousands of miles within weeks, then days, then hours, and now, when orbiting Earth, within minutes. That technological breakthrough launched a new epoch: the Anthropocene, so named to signify the impacts of human activities on a planetary scale within a geological timeframe.

The Industrial Revolution preceded the invention of photography and the motion picture. But it took a while for industrialization to cross oceans and continents. By the time steam-powered engines reached the Pacific Northwest, photography was a fledgling profession. Traveling with a wooden box containing his Long Focus Cycle Wizard Sr. camera, Asahel Curtis recorded the rise of industry, large-scale commercial agriculture, and new forms of transportation.

Curtis began his career shortly after the introduction of gelatin dry plates reduced the cost of photography and made it possible to capture objects in motion. The Washington State Historical Society archive of some fifty thousand Curtis negatives and prints shows mechanization at work in canneries, mills, wheat fields, logging operations, road-building, railroads, streetcars, and early attempts at manned flight. Over several decades, Curtis's camera recorded the transformation of lands, waters, and lives in Washington.

The images in the Curtis archive serve documentary makers as a resource for innumerable stories about his times. When the historical society created a permanent exhibit for the museum it built in Tacoma next to Union Station, the railroad terminal that brought forces of change to Washington, I used Curtis photographs in videos within the museum. To make Curtis's work more widely known, I scripted a documentary about Curtis himself. Randy Brinson and Stephen Hegg at KCTS, the Seattle PBS station, directed and produced it.[1]

Our challenge was to make this film more than an illustrated lecture with voice-over narration and representative quotes accompanying a succession of still photographs and ancient film clips. What was the story? Curtis was a booster, an advocate of unbridled progress. He was also an outdoors enthusiast, a lover of mountaineering who did not perceive the threat road-building might someday pose to the wildlands of Washington. This contrast lacked drama; for Curtis, like most of his contemporaries, thought nature too vast to be harmed by the works of humankind. The scenes of progress Curtis photographed represent a momentous historical upheaval. A show lacking dramatic conflict could not portray that interestingly or adequately.

As it happened, a personal conflict that shaped Curtis's life throws light on the historical transformation of his time. Asahel Curtis had a brother who was also a photographer: Edward Sheriff Curtis. The screenplay became a double biography, intertwining their lives for the show *Different Lenses*.

The Curtis family moved to Washington from Minnesota in 1887 when Edward was nineteen and Asahel thirteen. Soon thereafter, their father died. Edward, who had apprenticed as a photographer in St. Paul, joined a studio in Seattle. He and his business partner made portraits of wealthy patrons. But when the crash of 1893 ruined the economy nationwide, closing banks and factories and halting commerce, Edward lost his customers. With little to do in the studio, he took a camera outdoors. So began his lifelong fascination with American Indians. Edward met Princess Angeline, the daughter of Chief Sealth, for whom Seattle is named, and photographed her.

There was a market for such photos. With the Wounded Knee Massacre of 1890 marking the end of the Indian wars, citizens of a rapidly industrializing nation looked back on native people as noble emblems of an era that was receding from memory. Edward had the good fortune to encounter an expert on American Indians, George Bird Grinnell, while climbing Mount Rainier. Grinnell took him to the Blackfeet Reservation. There Curtis beheld the prairie "carpeted with tipis." Amazed by that encampment, Curtis found the purpose for the rest of his career: photographing Indians as a vanishing people.

Asahel began his career working in his brother's studio. In 1897, after the discovery of Klondike gold, Edward sent Asahel to the Yukon River. This was an arduous assignment. Asahel transported three thousand glass plates along with a ton of supplies over the Dead Horse Trail, named for the thousands of horses that died en route to the Yukon. The photographer was his own pack animal. He crossed the mountain pass repeatedly for weeks carrying provisions on his back.

During the two years he photographed and prospected, Asahel sent negatives home to Seattle. He did not learn until he returned that Edward had published the photos in a national magazine. Under his own byline, Edward wrote about the rush to the Klondike in the first person, as if he had made the journey. This infuriated Asahel. Edward's insistence on keeping the copyright in spite of Asahel's demand for ownership opened a breach between the brothers that lasted the rest of their lives. They did not speak at their mother's funeral. Their children grew up in the same city but never knew each other.

What makes their antagonism interesting beyond that bitter personal dispute is the fact that Edward and Asahel Curtis were each other's opposites as photographers. Photo historian Rod Slemmons makes this point in *Different Lenses*: "Asahel lived solidly in the present with a face toward the future. Edward Sheriff was standing in the present looking straight at the past. They were in effect standing back to back, one looking forwards, the other looking backwards."

The difference in their approach to photography gave the documentary a storyline as well as a title. One subject both men recorded is whaling by members of the Makah tribe, who live on the northwestern tip of the Olympic Peninsula. In 1910, Asahel's camera captured a Makah work crew skinning a whale on the shore of Neah Bay. The men wear workman's clothes of the time: trousers, shirts, jackets, and a variety of hats. Five years later, Edward photographed a Makah whaler holding a harpoon and two large sealskin floats. Wilson Parker is hatless; a skin covers his head, and a bearskin wrapped around his body conceals the pants he is wearing.

The truth in that photo is that Parker actually hunted whales; Makah traditions were relatively intact. That was not the case on other reservations Edward visited to photograph Indians. "What Curtis did," explains historian Richard White, "is take Indian people who have worked with and beside whites participating in the larger economy for their whole lives and dressed them up as these aboriginal relics who were fading away into the distance."

To support his project of portraying the timeless aborigine, Curtis turned to the richest, most powerful man in the country, J. P. Morgan. Morgan gave him the entire amount requested: seventy-five thousand dollars, a huge sum at the time. The tycoon was no lover of photographic art or of Indians. Curtis's portfolio served his interests. Railroads and other enterprises in Morgan's empire were driving native people from the land. By making people believe they were destined to disappear, Morgan turned the guilt of conquest into the romanticism of fate.

The myth of the vanishing race was not Curtis's creation alone, or J. P. Morgan's. It was fostered by the anthropology of their day, which sought to salvage the remnants of indigenous traditions—facts and artifacts as well as photos. Yet it is Edward Curtis's contribution that endures in the imagination. Even today, American Indians wearing contemporary clothes meet people who, on learning their background, are surprised and say, "You don't look like a real Indian." That is the power of photography and of cinematography: to replace knowledge and perception with images that seem more real than reality itself.

〇

The problems of how to look beyond an image that perpetuates a superficial impression and of how to reveal underlying historical forces dominated my first assignment for KCTS. Production executive Dave Davis called me in as the script doctor for a show that was part of a series about modern China. This episode, focusing on the Chinese economy, had been shot and was nearly completed in postproduction. It looked good. The only problem was it was boring.

The concept that guided the production seemed promising. China is making a transition from the Iron Rice Bowl, in which the government guarantees the necessities for living from womb to tomb, to a more open economy that offers opportunities for entrepreneurship and global trade. The central figure who epitomizes this change is a young woman who works for a cosmetics company. No longer dependent on the Iron Rice Bowl, she has a career promoting beauty products. And she is beautiful, a pleasure to behold. But she discloses little about herself; her makeup masks her personality. This image of perfection does not, in other words, reveal her character. She behaves but does not act. She is not interesting enough to hold an audience's attention for an hour.

The budget did not allow for any more production. The show had to be improved with the existing footage. I immersed myself in the outtakes and interview transcripts. It soon became clear that another approach to this subject was feasible, one that was illuminating. The production team had met the young woman's parents and her grandmother. Her parents, like almost everyone of their generation, were victims of the Cultural Revolution. The Maoists forced them to abandon their urban life for hard labor in the countryside. The grandmother had suffered during the Great Famine, which took the lives of tens of millions of Chinese between 1958 and 1961. To see that old woman cooking with care not to waste even one grain of rice is to glimpse the trauma her country endured. Seen as a member of a new generation just a few years after the massacre at Tiananmen Square, the young woman appears in a new light. Her ambition to prosper and to find security without support from the Iron Rice Bowl shines against the dark backdrop of starvation and disruption that her family managed to survive. This woman's self-concealment behind cosmetics, the very fact that she behaves perfectly and does not reveal her uniqueness in spite of the initiative she has taken in her career, represents the choice to conform that many members of her generation made in the wake of Tiananmen Square.

Dave Davis and his colleagues at KCTS liked this solution to the problem the show posed. But the executive producer of the series, who hired KCTS to make that segment on the Chinese economy, needed approval from Beijing for a feature film project that was in the works. There was no chance the Chinese government, which to this day bans public knowledge of the Great Famine within China, would tolerate the scenario I came up with. And KCTS would not revise the show under pressure of censorship.

✦

Script doctors take no Hippocratic Oath. Yet a triad of values governs documentary filmmaking. One is educational: to obtain and convey knowledge that increases public understanding. Another is esthetic: to work toward the highest possible production values, including quality sound and picture, and to tell stories well. The third is ethical. Ethical decision-making requires judgment applied to each case—for example, in representing each onscreen participant fairly.

The combination of inquiry, artistry, and ethics characterizes many personal lives but few professions. It found prominent expression at the dawn of the scientific era in the life and work of Leonardo da Vinci, who believed that "the eye is the window of the soul" and whose many contributions to science included the study of optics and the discovery that images enter the eye upside-down and are reversed in the brain. Da Vinci inspired Johann Wolfgang von Goethe, whose *Faust* sought knowledge at the cost of his soul and who, as a scientist, focused on light and the perception of colors. Immanuel Kant examined these three dimensions of value in his philosophical critiques, which examine what can be known, what should be done, and how one judges—an examination of esthetics that shaped Hannah Arendt's thinking about political judgment. Alexander von Humboldt, who became world-famous as an explorer and author in the early nineteenth century, considered nature, in its beauty and boundlessness, the fount of human freedom and progress. Those luminaries of the Enlightenment inspired the American transcendentalists Emerson and Thoreau, for whom "a true account of the actual is the rarest poetry,"[2] and Aldo Leopold, a great writer and pioneering conservationist. "Examine each question," wrote Leopold, "in terms of what is ethically and esthetically right as well as what is economically expedient. A thing is right when it tends to preserve the integrity, stability, and beauty of the biotic community."[3] One of the fields that carry forward the combination of knowledge, esthetics, and ethics is the making of museums, whose very name evokes the muses. Another is the art of documentary making. A beneficiary of the study of optics and of light, this field's most immediate predecessor was photojournalism.

Documenting the Industrial Revolution with his camera, Asahel Curtis based his career firmly upon the Enlightenment tripod of values. He was an artist, although some of his commercial photographs are made-to-order workmanship. The images he produced, many of which appeared in newspapers and magazines, increased public knowledge. And he was a man of personal as well as professional integrity.

Those values correspond to the ethos of an indigenous oral historian. Making *Native Heritage*, a video in the Washington history museum's permanent exhibit, with director Larry Johnson, I interviewed Vi Hilbert at her home. She lived between two airfields: Sea-Tac and Boeing Field. "About every thirty seconds there are airplanes," she complained. "And what am I doing at this time in my life? I'm a great-grandmother, preserving everything about the culture that it's possible for me to preserve, because if I don't, the coming generations won't have the benefit of the things that were left for me to pass on."

She stopped speaking as a plane passed by. "I am an Upper Skagit," Hilbert continued. "My mother and father were both traditional people from the Skagit River area. And because we are an oral tradition, all the important information of our people was committed to memory, and oral historians were given that responsibility. My father was one of those people. My mother was also. They were storytellers. They were genealogists. They were people who knew the importance of all the landmarks in our land: the rivers, the mountains, every hill. Everything had a name, and the people remembered those things.

"And the legends that they passed on give us the knowledge of who we are and how we happen to be here where we are. And we have always been here. The legends have told us this. So the legends to me are the most important part of our teaching, because the ancestors knew that this was where all information could be carried: the philosophy, the humor, the important things that a culture needs to maintain to keep it healthy and alive.

"Our historians, knowing the importance of committing to memory things that were important, could never deviate from the truth. That was one of the cardinal rules, that we are never to lie. And if in memorizing the important things from our culture, certain people were given that special responsibility for maintaining the integrity of a story or stories, then they couldn't deviate from the truth."

"Cut, there's a plane," said Bernie Krause, the sound recordist.

"How is knowledge actually passed on?" I asked once the sky was quiet again.

"Family members observe those young people who are responsible. Then they begin tutoring them. All elders then speak to this person who will be remembering. And because I am an only child, I was a part of the audience for every elder who spoke, knowing that I was required to listen. And this was in every kind of event: at the Shaker church, at travel meetings, at just overnight visits with friends and relatives. This is how we were trained: never just to run around playing outdoors when there were important things to hear.

"Listening is an important skill that many of our young people are not aware needs to be practiced. My people knew that when they were traveling out in the forest they had to listen to be keenly aware of all the things that were surrounding them in the forest. So this listening ability was practiced for safety as well as for remembering important historical things. My dad could listen to the water and know what was happening underneath the water. He could listen to the wind and know what was happening or what was going to happen."

"Wait," I said, hearing another airplane. When silence returned, Bernie Krause, listening through headphones, signaled to go ahead.

"My mother and dad were both storytellers, and their people before them were storytellers. My dad would tell me an X-rated story, and my mother would say, 'You're not going to tell her that story, are you?' I didn't know it was X-rated, and I listened to it, and just now at age seventy-seven I am realizing that some of these stories were X-rated that my dad told me.

"My Aunt Tusie is a good example of the perfect storyteller. She could become every character in the story. She could become the person who stood in the center of that story and draw a word picture for you of everything that was taking place. She made it live for you as she told it."

"Why was there such an emphasis on the oral tradition?" I asked.

"Because when you don't have a writing system," said Hilbert, "you have to be able to remember all the things that are important. And you sift through those things that are unimportant in order to remember those things that need to be taught to coming generations. And the people knew that. They didn't have references to go back to shelves and books on shelves. Their computers on top of their heads had to be plugged in all the time."

"Was there discussion about events as they happened, saying that this is something we're going to remember?"

"As an event happened," Hilbert replied, "for instance, when there was the big flood, when there was a log jam on the Skagit River, when there was an eclipse, people mentioned this as an important time period, because we had no calendar. My parents didn't know the month of their birth; they didn't know the year of their birth, because there were no calendars to mark that. My mother knew that she was about this age, and she was ten years younger than my dad. And he was born at a time when this took place. So they marked the periods of time by special events that everybody knew about.

"My mother and dad lived in my grandfather's longhouse, which was a communal home by the Skagit River. And my grandfather was the boss. What he said was law, and all the people knew that and abided by the very, very stern discipline that was administered in a home of this kind. For people to live together in harmony, there had to be discipline. And our people knew that and practiced it.

"My mother and dad got up every morning and went to the Skagit River to bathe. That was a rule, every morning, regardless of the weather.

"My dad was a canoe carver. Any time we needed transportation on the Skagit River or on the Baker River, he found a tree that could be used for a river canoe. Whole families could travel on a river canoe. As many as seven, eight people could travel with all their belongings. And when race canoes came into fashion, he knew how to create a race canoe that would be well-balanced and would be a winner.

"My mother and her grandmother lived in Edison Flats, which is saltwater area. Her grandmother, who raised her after her mother was killed in an accident, was very, very wise about earning a living in the saltwater area. So I have been told by my mother all the ways that my great-grandmother was able to utilize the saltwater area. She gathered oysters. She dug clams. She spear-fished in the Samish River, and those things were used then for barter."

This time, a change of videotape broke the flow of words. With the camera rolling again, Hilbert went on.

"From Eastern Washington on to the ocean, our people had ways different from each other. And because our people intermarried and had in-laws who were from eastern Washington and had in-laws who were from the ocean and from Canada, they learned the ways of all these people, knowing that there were differences. And when you are raised as a first person of this land, the very first rule you learn is about respect: respect for the people who live here, respect for the spirits who live here, respect for everything that has life. The essence of what they are teaching arrives at the same thing, and that's a respect for the gifts of the creator, human beings as well as plants and animals."

Asked where stories come from, Hilbert answered, "The wisdom of my ancestors. They knew that they couldn't just talk to people and have them listen. If they had something to say to them in a story, then people could listen. There was a lesson in every story."

And were the interpretations of a story left up to the people? "We wouldn't insult anybody by saying, 'You're too stupid to figure out what this story means to you. I have to tell you what it means to you.' How could I do that? The creator gave you a mind, a heart, to see things in your own special way. And so you will see that story however you choose to see it. And it's not right, and it's not wrong. It's the way you see it. That's important. We respect that. The creator gave you a mind that I'm going to respect, because you have something that the creator gave you that he didn't give me."[4]

The oral tradition, as Hilbert describes it, carries a responsibility to remember facts and convey truth. Its facts are often approximate; for example, the age of her parents. And its truth is culturally relative, like the assertion that the Upper Skagit people have always lived in their homeland. But while the facts in Hilbert's stories may not correspond to knowledge acquired through the written record and while scientific evidence concerning the migration of human beings around the planet contradicts indigenous accounts, the oral tradition remains distinct as well from pure fiction, which carries no burden of memory or responsibility for representing what is deemed to be the truth. In these respects, it is an antecedent of documentary storytelling.

The *Native Heritage* video, looping soundbites from the interviews with Hilbert and others, appears in its own theater in the Washington State History Museum. In dioramas around the permanent exhibit, more than ninety characters speak when their statue is approached or when one pushes buttons and screens to summon their words.[5]

One issue the makers of the museum debated was whether to guide viewers through the permanent exhibit with the aid of a directive floor plan and historical narration. They decided not to do this. Instead, people encounter the history that interests them, as it interests them. In doing so, they put themselves in the place of others, whoever they are, whenever they lived. This activity does not come naturally. According to E. O. Wilson, "The human brain evidently evolved to commit itself emotionally only to a small piece of geography, a limited band of kinsmen, and two or three generations into the future."[6] Recognizing the kinship of human beings that studies in paleontology, genetics, and linguistics describe scientifically, and that travel and communications around the Earth reveal experientially, expands the synaptic map within a human brain. Practicing within a museum what Arendt called "the inalienable right to go visiting"[7] is one way this occurs. Another way is seeing documentaries.

In addition to encountering predictable historical figures such as Lewis and Clark, visitors to the Tacoma museum find representative ancestors of the various communities in the Pacific Northwest. They came in wave after wave of migration, before, during and after the Industrial Revolution. The Paleolithic people who made the Clovis spearpoints displayed in the museum may have arrived separately from other bands that traveled to America during and after—and perhaps before—the last Ice Age. Indigenous languages spoken around Puget Sound and to the west, on the Olympic Peninsula, stem from language families as distinct as French and Chinese: the Makah speaking a Wakashan language and the Upper Skagit, Lushootseed, a Salishan language, while the Quileute and Chinook speak languages of entirely different kinds. In contrast with the Babel of their tongues, the similarity of the region's tribal cultures suggests long habitation and the irresistible influence of lands, waters, and wildlife on the ways that various groups of people live.

Touching a computer screen in a museum to hear sentences spoken in native Washington languages is a far cry from gaining knowledge carried in those vocabularies: place names, memories passed down, stories told. At least it suggests the linguistic riches of the preconquest Pacific Northwest. English enters the scene in diorama dialogues between tribal members and others—British explorer David Thompson and Jefferson's envoys, Lewis and Clark. These encounters occurred less than a century before cameras and phonographic cylinders existed and could have recorded them. Some of their lines come from oral histories and historic documents; some are imagined dialogue based on research, using Thucydides' method of having "speakers say what, in my opinion, was called for in each situation." As a result, past events appear in the present moment, and people who are distant in kind as well as in time become close at hand.

Images and voices represent these events and people in photo displays, videos, audio voices, and diorama sculptures across the exhibition floor. A pioneer farmwoman speaks with a miner and others at a general store in Walla Walla. "I was small when I first saw this valley," she says. "Our wagons stopped at the Whitmans' mission to rest." A Chinese work crew carves a railroad tunnel through the Cascades. Migrants from the Midwest, like the Curtis family, arrive at Union Station on one of the first trains into Tacoma. Ida asks, "Will Uncle Olaf meet us at the station?" "No, dear," says Birgitte. "He must tend his cows." Men are working at a shingle mill, with fingers missing. "Takes concentration. That's the main thing," says one man. "And fast hands." Freed slaves are literally railroaded into the state to displace striking miners. One of their descendants, a young man, encounters a former member of the Industrial Workers of the World (IWW), the union that organized migratory workers, in a Depression-era Hooverville shack. "Mind if I come in outa the rain?" he asks.[8] Japanese are transported to internment camps during World War II. "We went to Puyallup, or Camp Harmony, which had once been a fairgrounds," says a woman. "When we got there, I got sick to my stomach. I really did." A *bracero* sings a *corrido* about the hard times of apple harvesters. The migrations continue, generation after generation, to be remembered, or not, by descendants, to be represented, or not, in future exhibits, documentaries, and other forms of storytelling.

"One could say that hominids are born to travel," says the host in *Bridging World History*, a twenty-six-part series produced by Oregon Public Television. "From the beginning of the human story," Michael Pullen tells us, "people migrated vast distances, crossing oceans and inhabiting every continent, spreading outwards from the original African homeland." Genetic as well as fossil evidence "indicates that seven thousand five hundred generations separate contemporary human beings from the ancestors who lived in the savannas of eastern Africa."

Stories do not reach nearly that far back, but language may. "Was it the invention of language that made the great migrations possible," Pullen asks, "or was it the homo sapiens' migrations that made language necessary for survival?" The narrator imagines that "the ability of each human group to invent new things such as tools and songs and to teach these to their young could well have occurred as they encountered new environments while on the move."[9]

That journey has ended. People are everywhere. It is the global environment and relationships between groups of humans that are changing. The reach of our inventions, including media, and of our imaginations as we meet and tell stories, can bring us closer. Or drive us farther apart in spite of our increasing physical and virtual proximity in the Anthropocene.

PART THREE

THE NATURAL WORLD

We have been telling ourselves the story of what we represent in the land for 40,000 years. At the heart of this story, I think, is a simple, abiding belief: it is possible to live wisely on the land, and to live well.
—Barry Lopez

If you don't know the trees, you may be lost in the forest, but if you don't know the stories, you may be lost in life.
—Siberian Elder

◱ ON THE INTERSTELLARNET

Cosmology springs from the desire to comprehend the universe. Over the centuries before cosmology became a science, stories explained how the universe came to be: a cosmic egg cracking open; conflict between order and chaos; creation of cosmos from nothing; heaven and earth merging (or splitting apart); dismemberment of a primordial being; a changer who transforms everything.[1]

Some creation stories explain the origin of stars. In the constellation the ancient Greeks named Orion after a hunter in their mythology, three fishermen lifted into the sky in one of Vi Hilbert's Upper Skagit tales rise above stargazers every winter.[2]

In scientific cosmology, instead of people becoming stars, stars become people. All forms of life, the Earth, and all of the planets are made of stardust. All of the heavy elements—carbon, oxygen, nitrogen, the iron that reddens blood—form within stars and blast out into space when stars explode as supernovae. This is a phenomenal origin story, but how can one tell it? How does one show the origins of everything we are in events that display the kinship of all forms of life, not only here but throughout the cosmos?

Unlike those who heard stories of Orion many centuries ago, people of the twenty-first century have scientific information about the entire knowable universe. Yet we lack a sense of our place within the universe. Since Copernicus and Galileo overturned the belief that the heavens revolve around Earth, humanity has developed a more extensive, detailed, and accurate map of the universe than was ever possible before. Yet contemporaries lack a sense of meaning founded on that knowledge. We may know intellectually but not understand intuitively that we are creatures of the cosmos.

Stories can help us gain this understanding. To grasp reality requires imagination. "In the early stages of creation of both arts and science," wrote E. O. Wilson, "everything in the mind is a story."[3] A sense of meaning can grow, mindful of the big picture. But there is no picture, no cosmic egg, that could possibly bring home the evolving synthesis of scientific knowledge that places humanity's strutting and fretting on the stage of planet Earth within the contexts of deep time and deep space. The photos that opened minds toward a new understanding of existence, taken from Apollo expeditions to the Moon, show Earth *from* space: a uniquely beautiful life-bearing island in the void. No view from Earth into space evokes similar feelings.

"If the stars should appear one night in a thousand years," thought Ralph Waldo Emerson, "how would men believe and adore; and preserve for many generations the remembrance of the city of God which had been shown."[4] Yet even if stars did appear tonight for the first time in a millennium, the majority of the world's population, living in cities, would not see them. Light pollution cloaks celestial objects. Fortunately, the Earth herself has eyes, among them the twin Keck Observatory telescopes on Mauna Kea, the European Southern Observatory in Chile, and the orbiting Hubble, Fermi, and Chandra observatories. In this golden age of astronomy, images of and information about objects in space are available everywhere on the web at any time. The universe is visible on Earth as never before. And many of the myriad images are beautiful.

What is astonishing is both how much and how little our contemporaries know about the universe. Animal senses and intuition evolved in order to survive under varying conditions on Earth. Telescopes extended the range of what humans see beyond the biological horizon. Sir Isaac Newton realized, and spectroscopy revealed, that what eyesight observes is a minuscule fraction of light. Then in recent decades it became evident that all of the atoms in the universe, including those observed via wavelengths eyesight cannot see, from radio waves to X-rays, amount to less than 5 percent of the whole shebang. The rest of it, dark matter and dark energy, accounts for 27 percent and 68.3 percent respectively. Today, no one knows what dark matter consists of or what hidden force accelerates the expansion of space. These are mysteries, inspiring wonder and further inquiry. This transformation in humanity's sense of the universe took more than mathematics, experiments, observations, and technologies from telescopes to supercomputing. It took visionary leaps of the imagination.

These leaps have left the public in the dark. While science is cosmopolitan and its language universal, the data are typically obscure and the analysis that makes sense of them abstruse. To reach the public, images combined with the language of stories—metaphor, narration, character development, suspense—must come to its aid.

Joel Primack, a theoretical physicist who investigates dark matter, uses a metaphor to suggest where we stand in relation to the big picture. Primack likens human knowledge to an island and the unknown to the surrounding ocean. As the islanders add bits of knowledge to the ground on which they stand (here is iron, it comes from supernovae), the shoreline widens, but the mystery of what lies beyond endures.[5] Primack's wife, science writer/philosopher Nancy Abrams, extends this metaphor. The ocean, she imagines, is "dark energy, which fills the entire universe. On that ocean, there sail billions of ghostly ships made of dark matter. At the tops of the tallest masts of only the largest ships are tiny little beacons of light. Those beacons of light are what we see when we look out at the stars and galaxies in the universe."[6]

Primack and Abrams maintain that their metaphorical island in space is centrally located. It is not central in the way Earth was once believed to be, with humankind the measure of all things on a planet around which the entire cosmos revolves. But when one measures time and space cosmologically, they argue, humanity exists at a pivotal point. They want those whose timeframe is reckoned in human lifetimes rather than geological eras millions of years apart to consider the significance of being at the midpoint of the Sun's longevity, a 4.5-billion-year-old yellow dwarf star with five or six billion to go. They think it opportune that humans exist only 13.8 billion years since the Big Bang. This is soon enough to observe the entire universe before cosmic expansion pushes everything too far apart to perceive beyond the local galactic cluster. But these considerations are too remote to influence people at large.

Other arguments Primack and Abrams make for centrality focus on the human body. We, along with our surroundings, are made of the rarest materials in the universe, those star-cooked heavy elements. So is every planet and moon likely to harbor life. And our body's dimensions scale midway between the smallest possible measurement, the Planck length, and the largest thing we know, the visible universe. That is not just fortuitous, they explain. An intelligent species anywhere must have a body that is not too small to house abundant brains yet not too large for information to travel quickly throughout the organism. A real-life ET could be as small as a puppy, as large as a redwood tree. While this difference is huge for a human, it is insignificant on a spectrum ranging from the infinitesimal to the entire cosmos.

More germane to humanity's sense of our place in the universe is the nature of the human mind, which, like the cosmos, is impossible for anyone to know from an outside vantage point. That problem cannot be solved, but an insight gained through the craft of documentary storytelling can help: there is no time but the present. Just as light that comes from the Big Bang took 13.8 billion years to reach observers on Earth, just as the solar radiation that warms us took eight minutes to get here, any aspect of the past can be known only by what is present. What was present and now is past leaves in its wake facts, thoughts, and memories, but these scatter like parts of a dismembered god. What people recognize as reality are appearances—what appears to us. What filmmakers represent as reality via sounds and images that move on a lighted screen can be drawn only from what is available in the present—what the camera captures or a photo displays, what someone says or a book imparts, what a search engine pulls from the cloud. Those resources have to be assessed, organized, and interpreted in relation to each other. Whatever viewers grasp, be it a bit of trivia or a cosmological theory, depends on what they seek to know, on what is accessible for them to know, and on the extent of their receptivity here and now.

Each person's mind—and, collectively, human intelligence—is potentially the center of the universe because that is where everything at each moment converges. Through ourselves the universe is self-aware, yet for no one at any vantage point can that awareness be complete or fully comprehensive.

This understanding applies of course to intelligent observers anywhere.

࿐

Through the narrative device of a journey, storytellers take their audience wherever the story goes. In the thirteen-part PBS series *Cosmos*, Carl Sagan, riding a "ship of the imagination," transports viewers "billions and billions" of light-years through the universe.[7]

Sometimes the story itself is the outcome of a journey. Embarking on a new project, especially on an unfamiliar subject, opens the mind of a documentary screenwriter. For me, such a moment came in a call from NASA's Ames Research Center. Paul Langston was producing a documentary about the Kuiper Airborne Observatory. He hired me to write the script.[8]

The Kuiper, or KAO, was a telescope on wings: the telescope a thirty-six-inch Cassegrain reflector, the wings a C-141A cargo jet. On a typical working night between 1974 and 1995 (when it was retired), the cargo jet carried astronomers more than 41,000 feet over Earth's surface, above almost all of the atmospheric water vapor that obscures infrared radiation from space. Langston wanted his video to introduce high school students visiting NASA Ames to astronomy and to inform astronomers who were about to fly the KAO for the first time about the observatory's achievements.

An eye on the infrared universe extends knowledge of the cosmos considerably. The evolution of stuff, ranging from the ejecta of supernovae to the formation of interstellar clouds and the birth of stars and solar systems, becomes visible in infrared wavelengths. To capture photons of heat from afar, the KAO carried not only the telescope with an array of gyroscopes to keep it steady as the plane moved and a bank of computers to control the telescope's movements but also a Dewar cooling system—a tightly sealed cylinder injected with liquid helium that kept the detectors' temperature lower than eight degrees above absolute zero.

Comets carry clues to the evolution of everything. Packets of frozen cosmic dust left over from the formation of the solar system, they orbit from its outer reaches toward the Sun and, looping around the star, head back again. At times they crash into planets, as occurred sixty-five million years ago when an object about the size of Halley's Comet ended the dinosaurs' reign. The impact comets have on the evolution of life may be creative as well as destructive. In 1986, when Halley's Comet returned after seventy-five years to the vicinity of Earth, astronomers investigated this question from space and from the flying observatory. In the KAO, Harold Larson found spectra of water vapor, confirming the theory of Fred Whipple that comets are dirty snowballs. Wanting to know what the dirt was made of, Humberto Campins found "organic molecules, long carbon chains with hydrogen, nitrogen and other elements that are the raw material that is needed for life, but not life itself." Comets, he reasoned, "possibly contributed to the Earth's oceans" and mixed their organic compounds "in with that primordial soup."

The next year Comet Wilson was discovered. In search of new data, Campins and Diane Wooden scheduled flights on the Kuiper to the southern hemisphere to observe it. Just then a new point of light pierced the southern skies. This was for Wooden "an extraordinary cosmic event: the explosion of a massive star, releasing enough light to outshine an entire galaxy." Unlike the supernovae of 1572 and 1604, which exploded in the Milky Way, blazing brighter than any other star, Supernova 1987A brightened the Large Magellanic Cloud, a neighboring galaxy but far enough away that even a star outshining it impressed no one but astronomers. Supernova 1572, which amazed Tycho Brache, and Supernova 1604, appearing five years before Galileo first looked through a telescope, punctured the prevailing theory that the cosmos is fixed forever, consisting of eternally unchanging concentric spheres. The contemporary explosion of a blue giant star in the Magellanic galaxy offered Kuiper-borne astronomers an opportunity to test Stirling Colgate's theory about what the stuff blasted into space by supernovae is made of. It "was the first chance we had," said Wooden, "to really look all the way through a supernova and to explore throughout its infrared spectrum all the different elements which were ejected into the space around." Discovering the spectral lines of nickel, she taped a nickel onto her blackboard.[9]

The flight of the Kuiper that the viewers of the half-hour video would witness traveled east across the United States to the Mississippi River, then back west to its hangar in Mountain View, California. On board, along with the crew and the astronomers, were two high school science teachers and Edna DeVore of the SETI Institute (the Search for Extraterrestrial Intelligence). In each direction of travel, the telescope, looking out from the cargo jet's left side, scanned a different portion of the sky. As that night's targeted objects came into view, astronomers studying them received streams of data on their computer screens.

Besides telling the story of this journey, the KAO video opened an aperture onto the story of the universe. That night, Diane Wooden and Jackie Davidson had M42, the Orion Nebula, in their sights. They had equipped the telescope with a polarimeter to map the magnetic field of the stellar nursery. Wanting to know how stars are formed within a cloud of cosmic dust, they measured the direction in which dust grains oscillate there. That would indicate the alignment of the magnetic field, which affects the process of stellar birth.

The day of my flight to research the film prior to production, I parked in a large lot near the hangar and walked to a nearby building to meet Paul Langston and Edna DeVore. At some point, I realized my keys were missing. I searched near my car and around it and retraced my route to and from the building several times. NASA staff continued the search during our preflight meeting. Then it was time to board.

From inside, the Kuiper looked more like a ship than a plane, almost like a submarine whose periscope pointed to the stars. In flight, it was cold and noisy—a hard place to have a conversation. Nonetheless, I tried to interview a British astronomer. He was at a computer workstation looking at light the telescope captured from a quasar 4.5 billion light-years away. I kept thinking, the technology on this plane pinpoints an object in space a third of the way to the Big Bang, and I can't even find my keys in a parking lot.

We landed at 3:00 AM. Since I could not drive home, Edna DeVore took me to her place in San Jose. There I rested and waited until my wife could send me another set of keys. And I read a book: *Is Anyone Out There? The Scientific Search for Extraterrestrial Intelligence* by Frank Drake.[10]

In *Cosmos*, Carl Sagan speculates about the existence of living things on other worlds. But that series touches on many other subjects as well.

I thought that the science of extraterrestrial life deserved a series of its own. This was a matter of self-knowledge; for if life is truly universal, we have only one sample, the carbon-based life that evolved from a common ancestor during the last 3.5 billion or so years, to consider. How it originated and where it came from, whether life emerged on Earth or arrived on a meteor or comet, are unanswered questions. As for intelligent alien life, it was worth considering what intelligence is and what forms it might take elsewhere. Images of aliens in science fiction draw more from fiction than from science, being either obviously modeled on the human prototype, like the invaders in *The Day the Earth Stood Still*, or based on terrestrial creatures that shock hominids, like the towering insect of *War of the Worlds* and the gigantic octopus-like, cosmonaut-grabbing beast from *Planet Berg*. Here was an instance in which nonfiction could be not only stranger but far more interesting than fiction.

Frank Drake's book *Is Anyone Out There?* unveils an equation that assesses the odds for the existence of extraterrestrial intelligence in this galaxy. The Drake Equation assembles the relevant factors, such as the number of stars; the fraction of stars that have planets; the number of planets that can potentially support life; the fraction of those where life takes hold; of those, the fraction where intelligent life develops; and of those, the fraction of civilizations whose technologies send detectable signs of their existence into space. The last factor, L, is the longevity of a civilization advanced enough to produce interstellar messages.

L raises questions whose answers are incalculable: can technological civilizations avoid self-destruction long enough to communicate across the cosmos? And is there something inherently self-destructive about civilizations that have the capacity to become technologically advanced? Events of the twentieth century—totalitarian rule, total war, genocide, and the development of weapons of mass destruction—made these questions unavoidable. The thought of entirely different forms of intelligent life took this inquiry out of the all-too-familiar context of recent history, focusing instead on the fundamental characteristics of intelligence and of the technologically advanced civilization an intelligent creature might create. This was a crucial matter of self-knowledge.

Two such characteristics came to mind.

First, the defining ability of a "rational animal" is symbolic thought. Intelligence generates symbols such as the images painted on the walls of Lascaux and Chauvet, which are representative, and the language used to describe them, which is abstract. Representative symbols evoke emotional and spiritual responses; they can be charged with depths of meaning. The abstraction of symbols from their contexts makes education possible over great distances and long spans of time; it gives the development of skills such as tool-making continuity within a vast variety of circumstances, as when a species migrates around a planet.

According to historian Yuval Noah Harari, *Homo sapiens'* ability to create "imagined realities" enabled our human ancestors to prevail over *Homo neanderthalensis*.[11] According to Erik H. Erikson, "Man could endow himself with pelts, feathers and paints, and eventually costumes and uniforms—and his universe with tools and weapons, roles and rules, with legends, myths and rituals, which served to bind his group together and endow its unique identity with that super-individual significance which inspires loyalty, heroism, and poetry."[12] When civilizations form, people from various tribes, speaking different languages, manage to organize themselves with the use of symbolic objects such as icons, coins, and flags. Authorities can arouse passionate attachment to those objects regardless of experience, wisdom, or common sense.

Second, the defining characteristic of an advanced technological civilization is the ability to use forms of energy external to the organic body to move machines and other objects. As these forms of energy become more abundant and the machines more powerful, organized groups' ability to destroy their adversaries and civilization's ability to alter its environment can increase exponentially.

Put these two characteristics together, and one finds an inherent potential for self-destruction, as when the combination of nationalism and nuclear weapons made the threat of annihilating people by the millions, incinerating their lands, and thrusting radioactive clouds into the atmosphere seem rational to the leaders of superpowers and their followers. These two characteristics together also make movies and computers possible: both are energy-driven mind machines. Another consequence is the potential of an advanced civilization to communicate with places beyond its home planet or moon. An extraterrestrial civilization that has existed long enough to send and receive messages via some Interstellarnet might have acquired the wisdom needed to cope with the challenge of its capacity for self-annihilation; either that, or the civilization achieved near immortality through a combination of artificial intelligence and robotics.

The subject of extraterrestrial intelligence inspires reflections of this kind, but first things first. For there to be intelligent life on other worlds, there has to be life. And what is required for life to exist, here or elsewhere? What *is* life? To explore these questions, I initiated a film project that became the two-part series *Life Beyond Earth*: the first part about life and its boundary conditions, the second about the search for intelligent life elsewhere in the universe.

Doing preliminary research into Part One while writing the first proposal for this project, I encountered a field of knowledge previously unknown to me: the hybrid science of astrobiology.

For a documentary screenwriter, ignorance is a virtue. Learning about something for the first time, one looks at it freshly, without preconceptions. Every documentary must answer the viewers' question, "So what—why should I watch this?" I find my answer in whatever excites my interest. If it can sustain me for months or years, it is likely to interest the public as well. The appetite for knowledge resulting from that discovery makes the questions I ask people I interview sincere, and they respond in kind.

Still, my ignorance of astrobiology indicated not only a lack of knowledge but also the reluctance of scientists to publicize what they do. Interviewing scientists for other programs, I had found it difficult to extract statements that were usable as sound bites. Answering my questions, some were, in effect, speaking a foreign language as they translated their thinking from equations and technical terms into common speech. Another difficulty was that scientists often qualified their remarks with unnecessary details and reservations. Linus Pauling, whom I interviewed in 1982, was exceptional; when asked for a thirty-second version of an elaborate remark, he provided exactly that without any jargon; but by that time Pauling had been giving interviews for half a century.

Too many members of the scientific community are, I believe, unwilling to describe their work in terms that are accessible to the public. Some fear the scorn of colleagues who condemn popularizers—a scorn that was directed at Carl Sagan even though he was an accomplished scientist as well as a celebrity.[13] As a consequence, scientists bear some responsibility for public ignorance of their fields, from biology to astrobiology. That ignorance of basic facts and established theories impairs the ability of citizens to participate intelligently in a democracy. It also alienates people from the life around us and the universe at large, keeping us apart from nature although we are part of it. By making science accessible through storytelling, documentaries can, to some extent, turn ignorance into curiosity and curiosity into knowledge.

To initiate a documentary series is a daunting task, especially for an independent media professional. A lot of money has to be raised and a production team assembled. In this case, the time was ripe and the right people available to obtain the needed support. I wrote Dave Davis at the Seattle PBS station KCTS. He contacted an international distribution company, Devillier Donegan Enterprises, which had a coproduction deal with PBS. As executive producers, Ron Devillier and Brian Donegan wanted someone well known associated with this project to give it credibility and to help them sell the show. I invited Timothy Ferris, a science writer, to join us and script the series.

An amateur astronomer since his childhood in Florida, Ferris keeps an eye on the universe from a private observatory at his homestead on Sonoma Mountain in California. On the fourth of April 1997, as Comet Hale-Bopp brightened while approaching Earth, having passed perihelion, the closest it will get to the Sun for more than four thousand years, Ferris threw a party at Rocky Hill Observatory. He retracted the rolling roof and tilted the telescope toward the sky. Guests looked through the eyepiece at a strange feature around the comet's nucleus, a spiral pattern. Our host ventured an explanation, later confirmed by Hubble imaging, that "the spiral was the result of a single, robust jet shooting out dust from the spinning nucleus, like water from a lawn sprinkler."[14] In other ways, Hale-Bopp was like all comets, an iceberg in space transporting evidence of the origins of the solar system. We who watched it carried within us, in every atom, offspring from the beginning of time, a realization expressed in Ferris's books *Coming of Age in the Milky Way* and *The Whole Shebang*.

Ferris was a writer for *Rolling Stone* magazine when he met and interviewed Carl Sagan. They became friends. When Sagan planned a series of phonograph records conveying images as well as sounds as the interstellar equivalent of a message in a bottle for NASA's Voyager probes, Ferris and Frank Drake belonged to his small circle of advisors.

Voyagers 1 and 2 would gather data from Jupiter, Saturn, Uranus, and Neptune before traveling, at speeds approaching forty thousand miles per hour, in opposite directions into interstellar space. They became the first human-made objects to escape the gravitational pull of the solar system. Were aliens ever to open the time capsules in the Voyager probes that were launched from Earth in 1977, they would find, on the discs that were dubbed "the Golden Record," nature sounds and greetings in fifty-five languages, varieties of music ranging from Beethoven to Chuck Berry, and 118 images, including a diagram of the solar system, silhouettes of a naked man and woman, and a photo of a mother breastfeeding her baby.

The contents of those time capsules, which will pass neighboring stars no sooner than seventy thousand years from now, were difficult to choose. The producers of the Golden Record had many conversations, arguments, and listening sessions as they considered what would interest extraterrestrials. Interviewed by Sagan's biographer, Keay Davidson, Ferris recalled, "A lot of things were played that one or the other of us would say, 'Why are we listening to this crap?' and someone would say, 'Wait a minute. There's something here.'"[15]

In the 1980s, Ferris wrote and starred in a PBS documentary about cosmology, *The Creation of the Universe*. Its closing scene mirrors the opening scene of *Cosmos*: Ferris on the shore speaking about the universe as the ocean surging behind him suggests mysterious depths. In contrast to Sagan, who regarded religion as the adversary of science, Ferris sought to show their compatibility. Regarding the first nanosecond of cosmic evolution, Ferris recites the opening of *Genesis*. After visiting Fermilab in Illinois, he takes us to the Gothic cathedral in Beauvais, France, that inspired the design of Fermilab's twin-towered headquarters. Throughout, Ferris emphasizes the mystery that transcends scientific knowledge. In the concluding scene, he quotes Einstein's aphorism that the most incomprehensible thing about nature "is that it is comprehensible." Then Ferris asks, "What is there about the human mind that resonates with the rest of the universe that we're able to understand anything about the workings of nature on the largest scale?"

This is a mystery especially when one considers that before humans developed thermonuclear technology, replicating the force that fuels the stars, all of the forces harnessed to extend the abilities of primate bodies—fire, wind, water, and electromagnetism—were terrestrial. If the goals of evolving life forms are survival and reproduction, how could the human mind have grasped a stellar sword of Damocles that disrupts evolution itself? Hominids have three-dimensional perception, and that, combined with the use of tools, worked wonders from navigation to industrialization. So when Bernhard Riemann developed a four-dimensional geometry, was this his invention, a product of pure reasoning? Or was it a discovery by a mind attuned to the universe? Surely the nineteenth-century mathematician did not imagine that his non-Euclidian geometry would make scientific cosmology possible. Surely Einstein had no idea that by adding a cosmological constant to the four-dimensional equations of the general theory of relativity he would enable future scientists to measure dark energy. Instead, he thought that this constant, which he added to keep the universe from collapsing before he learned it is expanding, was his greatest blunder. Were Riemann and Einstein describing the universe or was the universe describing itself through them?

One can say that mind, like the body, is made of cosmic stuff and that the universe is no less where we are than "out there." One can consider with Spinoza "the union existing between the mind and the whole of nature."[16] One can declare, like Emerson, that "the Universe is the externalization of the soul"[17] or claim, like Christof Koch, "that "consciousness is a fundamental feature of the universe."[18] These thoughts do not answer the question; they leave the mystery intact, the ocean surrounding the island of knowledge unfathomed. On the boundary between science and the unknowable, storytelling sounds the depths.

Ferris uses metaphors to illuminate his subject. In one sequence, he walks up the spiral staircase of a lighthouse—or its TV studio equivalent. Each step represents a fraction of the first billion years since the Big Bang. Along the way, Ferris opens windows to depict what appeared in the universe at different stages of its early evolution—a protogalaxy like the Milky Way, the birth of atoms, the "soup of free quarks"—back to the first instant of time when everything was infinitesimally small. While much of his PBS documentary *The Creation of the Universe* is an illustrated lecture interspersed with sound bites, this scene is inspired.

In developing the new series *Life Beyond Earth*, Ferris and I intended to employ all of the tools of documentary storytelling. Research included a weekend gathering of scientists and filmmakers at a resort, Isis Oasis in Sonoma County. At first glance, this was a bizarre place for a retreat to plan a science documentary. Isis Oasis has a temple to Isis and a theater where light streams through stained-glass windows depicting images from ancient Egypt. But the Egyptians were astute observers of the cosmos. Their word for iron, which they used for tools and beads, means "metal of heaven." They situated pyramids according to the cycles and positions of the Sun and stars. Ptolemy, whose theory of concentric spherical heavens combined Aristotle's cosmology with astronomical observations, was a citizen of Roman Egypt.

Within the theater, we discussed studies of the habitable zone for life on Earth. This is also known as the Goldilocks zone, where conditions are not too hot and not too cold, but just right to harbor life. The places where "extremophiles" manage to exist range from sulphuric thermal vents deep within the Pacific Trench to ice-laden Antarctic lakes. The Goldilocks zone on this planet provides parameters for the prospects of finding life on Mars and other places in the solar system. One possibility is Europa, a moon of Jupiter whose icy surface may cover an ocean heated by the satellite's molten core. Another is Titan, a moon of Saturn. The Voyager probes revealed that Titan has a dense atmosphere rich in hydrocarbons. The basic requirements for life as we know it are few: liquid water, organic chemicals, and a source of energy. This combination exists elsewhere in the solar system, and given that billions of stars with solar systems of their own whirl around billions of galaxies, life is likely to be widespread across the universe.

The research retreat offered an opportunity to do covert casting. Some of the scientists who attended were potential interviewees for the program. In addition, we asked them to recommend people to interview who had not come to Isis Oasis.

Identifying great "characters" can be all-important in documentary filmmaking. To find scientists who are personally engaging and able to convey their knowledge clearly to the general public is a tall order. Nor can everyone who has these qualities be their best in front of a camera. Having Ferris as an on-camera narrator gave this series the option to rely on his talent when few others could fill the bill.

During preproduction, to generate and organize content for the series, Ferris and I used a low-tech method that still beats software. Everything we thought of including got written on an index card. The cards were arranged and rearranged in various combinations on a bulletin board. They were color-coded: white for points the narrator might make, red for special effects, other colors for scenes on location, interview sound bites, and so on. At a glance, the arrangement of cards on the vertical surface shows the emerging structure of the series along with its contents and the relative proportions of its elements. Take red cards, for example. As a producer, I wanted few special effects. They are expensive.

To scout a possible location, we drove to the Dish, a radio telescope in the hills above the Stanford campus. It had been used to study Earth's atmosphere, to communicate with spacecraft and satellites, and to transmit signals to the Voyager probes. Ferris had the brilliant idea of transmitting a *Life Beyond Earth* sequence from the Dish to a planet orbiting 70 Virginis, a sun-like star sixty light-years away.

When originally discovered, the planet, called 70 Virginis b, was thought to move within the star's habitable zone. Subsequently, it was found to have an eccentric orbit, bringing b periodically very close to 70 Virginis and making it therefore too hot for living things as we know them to exist.

70 Virginis b was among the first extrasolar planets to be discovered. Since then, thousands have been identified, most of them massive, since the largest planets are most easily observed. But smaller, Earth-sized worlds have also been found. Astronomers estimate that there could be forty billion of them orbiting within the habitable zones of stars within the Milky Way. If a transmission via radio telescope were planned at this writing, there would be hundreds of Earth-like planets, detected by the Kepler Space Telescope, to choose from, the closest only twelve light-years distant.

By now, people on other worlds may have already seen terrestrial TV. Electromagnetic signals from every broadcast that has ever occurred radiate outward from Earth in a sphere exceeding ninety light-years in radius. Already this mediasphere surrounds hundreds of thousands of stars and continues to reach more as it expands at the speed of light. The inhabitants of a planet orbiting one of those stars may have detected these signals and deciphered *The Howdy Doody Show*, *See It Now*, and *Star Trek*.

The idea of a targeted broadcast via radio telescope was different. Like the Golden Record, this would be a deliberate message. Earth's inhabitants could await a response after the number of years it would take for light to travel to the exoplanetary audience and to come back. In effect, *Life Beyond Earth* would establish Earth's website on the Interstellarnet: a locus for gathering information and for sending and receiving communications. This idea raises the intriguing question that has long been pondered by proponents of SETI: what kind of message could species from different worlds exchange with one another? Music and nature sounds, the biophony of animal voices? Or 3-D biological imaging—neural charts of the brain, for example? Works of art and mathematics? Scientific theories? What about stories? What would our stories be, and in which language or with which graphics would we share them? If we played an alien's equivalent of the Golden Record, would we enjoy it? Would we understand anything?

Ferris proposed a live five-minute presentation at the end of the series in which people everywhere on Earth are able to send audio, video, and written messages toward the extrasolar planet. A random switching device would allow this experiment to occur spontaneously, without editorial control. It would be an impromptu presentation of human life at that instant in time. The show would conclude by anticipating the response from 70 Virginis b. Would aliens there merely change the channel? If they answered, this venture would have discovered a New World, transforming humanity's understanding far more than Columbus's trip across the pond.

Besides being an experiment in extraterrestrial communications, this sequence promised to be a stellar example of the documentary's ability to "show not tell," to illustrate and dramatize its subject. Unfortunately, Ferris's idea did not survive the scrutiny of lawyers. I learned that the United Nations Office for Outer Space Affairs does not allow a targeted interstellar broadcast. The UN Treaty on Principles Governing the Activities of States in the Exploration and Use of Outer Space, including the Moon and Other Celestial Bodies, holds the states that are parties to the treaty responsible for "national activities in outer space . . . whether such activities are carried out by governmental agencies or by nongovernmental entities." That was us: a nongovernmental entity. But responsible for what? If 70 Virginis b is sixty light-years away, then 120 years after the transmission, an alien's reply might have detrimental effects, though it is hard to imagine effects more detrimental than are caused by existing television programs, political campaigns, and commercial advertising. Besides, if *Life Beyond Earth* were either to anger those creatures or make Earth seem desirable to invade, their punitive and/or plundering space flotilla would be in transit for thousands of years after they receive this incitement from Earth. Attorneys are necessarily risk-averse, but this call went beyond all bounds of credibility. Science fiction, once again, triumphed over facts, fantasy over common sense.

I found it interesting that this fantasy projects humanity's propensity to conquer new worlds onto our expectations of other "intelligent life." One argument supporting the idea that "we are alone"—in space, that is, as if there were no other intelligent life on Earth—is Fermi's question, "Where are they?" If there are billions of planets and moons in our galaxy on which intelligent life forms may have evolved and billions of years during which aliens could have explored the galaxy, why has no one shown up; no one, that is, whose visit has been proven beyond a doubt?

E. O. Wilson has an intriguing answer to Fermi's paradox: "Perhaps the extraterrestrials just grew up. Perhaps they found out that the immense problems of their evolving civilizations could not be solved by competition among religious faiths, or ideologies, or warrior nations. They discovered that great problems demand great solutions, rationally achieved by cooperation among whatever factions divided them. If they accomplished that much, they would have realized that there was no need to colonize other star systems. It would be enough to settle down and explore the limitless possibilities for fulfillment on the home planet."[19]

Even had we aimed the series at an inhabited world, the target audience might have ignored it, being busy exploring possibilities for fulfillment. The challenge that every storyteller faces, engaging an audience, could have been insurmountable in this case, and the absence of a reply would have proven nothing except that there is life beyond television.

THE VIEW FROM THE SIERRA MADRE

On 31 October 2011, the birth of a child caused the world population to reach seven billion. Fittingly, this occurred on Hallowe'en, a scary holiday. We contemporaries draw more resources from planet Earth than can be sustained. More than a billion people lack a renewable source of fresh water. The oceans are overfished. Coral reefs are dying as the ocean acidifies. The atmosphere is increasingly polluted with greenhouse gases. On land, deforestation, soil erosion, the spread of built environments, the shrinking of wildlife habitats, and the consequent extinction of species cumulatively diminish the self-renewing capacity of the biosphere.

Like the nuclear crisis, the unraveling of Earth's life-support systems due to human activities is hard to contemplate. Documentaries that address this subject run the risk of frightening people into responding with an intensity that cannot be sustained while driving others to despair. The headline for a review of a five-part series about environmental history calls it a "documentary so honest you'll want to kill yourself."[1]

A no-less-honest but emotionally tolerable storyline responds to these questions: what can people do to reverse humanity's negative impacts on life, and how can those actions enrich our spirits as well as improve our situation? There are many answers and many stories to tell along those lines.

For me, an approach to fixing the world came into focus while researching and scripting *Green Fire: Aldo Leopold and a Land Ethic for Our Time*.

During the years that I worked on *Green Fire*, I found that few of my friends, no matter how well educated or knowledgeable, had heard of Aldo Leopold. That was striking since, to my mind, Leopold ranks with Henry David Thoreau and John Muir as a preeminent American naturalist. The ecological wisdom Leopold applied to the tasks of conservation, wildlife management, erosion control, watershed management, sustainable agriculture, and ecosystem restoration can guide the understanding and transform the worldview of our contemporaries. Leopold, who died in 1948, was not only ahead of his time, he is still ahead of ours.

Green Fire: Aldo Leopold and a Land Ethic for Our Time originated as a biography of Leopold. The director, Steve Dunsky, and the editor, Ann Dunsky, agreed with me that he deserves to be as well known as Thoreau and Muir; the film could help make his name a household word. The Aldo Leopold Foundation, which was founded by his children and whose director, Buddy Huffaker, joined the project as executive producer, shared this goal. But ALF was not interested in making a biopic. The foundation wanted the subject of *Green Fire* to be Leopold's legacy, the contemporary application of his work.

I understood the concern about a strictly biographical film. Only a few seconds of footage of Leopold exist, and although he was often on the radio, no recording of his voice has been found. A film that told his story as a historical character would rely on still photos, archival footage, talking heads, and narration—a standard documentary formula that can be boring—whereas viewers would appreciate and might emulate people in a film who, inspired by Leopold's land ethic, connect urbanites with the countryside, make farming and ranching sustainable, conserve ecosystems, restore wildlife habitat, and bring species back from the brink of extinction.

But to do that was problematic from the perspective of documentary storytelling. How can one make a film about the land ethic today without telling Aldo Leopold's story? His legacy exists in so many fields across the landscape—from cities to suburbs, from ranches and farmlands to wilderness—that the film would have no focal point for those who do not know Leopold. Somehow, *Green Fire* would have to combine his biography with contemporary scenes. That too was a challenge. How would we connect the career of a man who died in 1948 with work people are doing in many places, of many kinds, today? Have them speak about Leopold's influence? Recall the first time they read his book, *A Sand County Almanac*? In production, Steve Dunsky obtained many statements of that kind. On Ann Dunsky's editing screen they fell flat, proving the adage "show not tell" by displaying its flip side.

Luckily for us, one of Leopold's biographers, Curt Meine, is a conservation biologist, and he knows many people and organizations whose work is inspired and informed by Leopold. Meine is an engaging presence on camera, as the Dunskys and I learned while making *The Greatest Good*, a two-hour documentary history of the US Forest Service.[2] We realized that Curt could tell Leopold's story as the voice-over narrator and appear on camera visiting people who cultivate his legacy.

But giving him that role still did not solve the problem of presenting the variety of Leopold-related fields without the film losing its focus, nor did it ensure that the biographical part of the movie would keep viewers interested.

Four additional decisions gave the film the unity and vitality it needed. We have Leopold address the viewer through the voice of Peter Coyote, an actor whose understanding of conservation runs deep. We show contemporary legacy sequences that take place within regions where Leopold lived and worked, aiding transitions from the life to the legacy. We focus on Leopold's guiding idea, the land ethic, as the theme that weaves all aspects of the film together. And our storyline renews a famous story Leopold told: his account of seeing a fierce green fire in the eyes of a dying wolf.

It was our luck that, during the production of the documentary, a previously unknown letter Leopold wrote to his family about the incident in which he saw that "fierce green fire" was discovered in a safe deposit box. It provided clues that enabled Curt Meine and Susan Flader, who is also a Leopold scholar, to identify the time and place of his shooting of the wolf. Having Leopold describe the event voice-over as we show Meine, Flader, and forester Don Hoffman looking out over the fateful rimrock exactly a hundred years later makes that iconic moment vivid and moving.

Adding to the drama, it so happened that thanks to the reintroduction of Mexican wolves in that region, there was a wolf pack nearby. Long after the "varmint eradication" campaign that Leopold actually championed in his early days, the biotic community of Apache National Forest is being restored. "For one species to mourn the death of another is a new thing under the sun,"[3] Leopold wrote about passenger pigeons, whose flocks once filled Midwestern skies. It is also a new thing under the Sun for one species to save another from extinction, as has occurred with Mexican wolves, sandhill and whooping cranes, condors and other creatures, thanks to conservation biology and wildlife management, two of the applied sciences that Leopold pioneered.

The Dunskys and I grappled with the problem of how to structure the wolf story. One idea, to open with animation of a howling wolf, its green eyes blazing, had the virtue of capturing viewers' attention at a visceral level but ran the risk of distorting expectations of what the show was about. We decided to give Leopold's story structural prominence, dividing the sequence into three parts, one in each act.

Leopold had the poet's gift of metaphor—"green fire" is a striking example, and many of his sentences are aphorisms. In the film, we hear his words during contemporary as well as biographical sequences; for what Leopold wrote means as much today as when he lived. For example: "Our tools are better than we are, and grow better faster than we do. But they do not suffice for the oldest task in human history: to live on a piece of land without spoiling it."[4]

These words are food for thought. On the page they rest, open for reflection. But in a film, they go by quickly, and the medium moves one's attention to the next sequence. That limitation is inherent to a motion picture. The makers of *Green Fire* can only hope audience members are moved by the film to read Leopold and learn from him directly.

There are so many ways to show Leopold's legacy in action that the documentary had a wide variety of scenes to choose from in places where he lived and worked: Iowa, where Leopold spent his boyhood; the Southwest, where he began his career with the Forest Service; and Wisconsin, where he taught wildlife management and practiced ecosystem restoration.[5]

On land near the family shack in "sand county" Wisconsin, Leopold's daughter Nina does scientific research on skis. "Dad," she tells us, "took phenological records. He was recording the natural events of the season: the first blooming of plants, the arrival of birds, and so forth. And so, here I am, age ninety-one; guess what I'm doing." Nina Leopold Bradley kept track of about 350 items. This data, which the family has recorded since the mid-1930s, is invaluable for tracking the impacts of climate change.

On his ranch in New Mexico, Sid Goodloe, wearing a cowboy hat, rides his horse. He is the very image of a Westerner. "We were out here to conquer this country, not to make it better," says Goodloe. Speaking of his conservation practices, Goodloe remarks that a steward of the land "manages his ecosystem holistically, and he shares that knowledge with other people." It is convincing to hear a successful rancher say this, even if he talks like an environmentalist.

What nonfiction film does not often do well is portray an organization within the context of a larger story. That can require lengthy exposition, for it is harder to characterize an organization than to show a person or a small group on the screen. And having presented it, one has to transition back to the main story, which can be cumbersome. We had to resign ourselves, as filmmakers, to this limitation even though Leopold's legacy of ecological coalition building is well represented in the Southwest. In an essay, Courtney White, a leader of the Quivara Coalition, describes a movement he calls the new agrarianism, which "includes a dynamic intermixing of ranchers, farmers, conservationists, scientists, and others who aim to create a regenerative economy that works in harmony with nature." According to White, "Leopold is the spiritual mentor of this hopeful effort."[6] To show that would require a film in itself.

The conservation organization in the Southwest that the film does refer to, but only in passing, is the Malpai Borderlands Group. Rancher Bill McDonald, who is in the film, intercut with Goodloe, belongs to Malpai. But all we see is a photo of a meeting as McDonald, on horseback, says, "It would always come down to personal relationships and trying to get folks to work together to try to create a future that includes open space and healthy functioning systems." The fact that a grassroots, landowner-run group is coordinating ecosystem management on almost a million acres of federal as well as private land goes beyond the frame of reference of the Leopold film, even though as a forester, Leopold initiated collaboration between ranchers and his federal agency in the Southwest. Malpai has too many components over too large a landscape to be contained within the frame of *Green Fire*.

The movie tracks Leopold's path toward his central idea, the land ethic. In doing so, it makes use of his talent as a storyteller. The story about the wolf that he recounts in his essay "Thinking Like a Mountain" dramatizes that idea and gives it an iconic metaphor: green fire. "I was young then and full of trigger-itch," Leopold wrote, looking back on the killing of a mother wolf at the beginning of his career with the Forest Service. Seen in retrospect, when Leopold, near the end of his life, wrote the essays in *A Sand County Almanac*, his encounter with the wolf seems like an epiphany. "We reached the old wolf in time to watch a fierce green fire dying in her eyes. I realized then, and have known ever since, that there was something new to me in those eyes—something known only to her and to the mountain."

The relationship between that story and the concept of the land ethic is not self-evident. What Leopold wrote was that something new was revealed, something unknown to him. He went on to say what he thought at the time, that "fewer wolves meant more deer, . . . no wolves would mean hunters' paradise."[7]

That was the view he acted on to great effect in subsequent years. In 1915, six years after he began working with the Forest Service in New Mexico and Arizona, Leopold organized Game Protective Associations. Sportsmen who joined them supported the eradication of predators of game animals. In an article published in the *Pine Cone*, the bulletin of the New Mexico GPA, Leopold called for "the reduction of predatory animals . . . the wolves, lions, coyotes, bob-cats, foxes, skunks, and other varmints."[8] He himself did not take part in "varmint" hunts. In those years, the forester was under doctor's orders while recovering from nephritis, an acute inflammation of the kidneys that almost killed him.

But as one of the leaders of the government's antipredator campaign in the region, Leopold bore responsibility for the killing of grizzly bears, mountain lions, and wolves in the mountains of the Southwest.

His efforts to protect game animals and increase their numbers expanded the mission of the Forest Service. When Gifford Pinchot created the agency in 1905, during the presidency of his friend Theodore Roosevelt, wood was as important a resource for the United States as oil is today. The building of cities and factories, ships and railroads, the energy they burned, the ties for the train tracks, the everyday necessities of cooking and heating, all required abundant supplies of wood. Cut-and-run deforestation threatened the growth of the United States. Establishing public lands and managing them so that wood could grow as a renewable crop over the long run was the conservationists' response to this crisis. What Leopold realized as a Forest Supervisor was that the best criterion for the success of forestry was not just the number of trees or the quantity of board feet, but its overall effect on the land; he also realized that game, soil, and water were other "crops" of the national forests that served the public interest. But no one understood at the time the interrelationship of all the factors that made the life of a forest renewable.

During the 1920s, an advance that increasingly endangered wildlife and wild lands was road building. Roads did more than bring hunters to previously inaccessible areas in the Southwest; they also cut through those lands, damaging animal habitats. As deer populations increased in the mountains of Arizona and New Mexico, Leopold thought that maintaining a large roadless area would safeguard the recreational promise of backcountry hunting trips. "Wilderness," he wrote, "is the one kind of playground that man can not build to order. I contrived to get the Gila headwaters withdrawn as a wilderness area to be kept as pack country, free from additional roads forever."[9] This initiative, setting aside the Gila Wilderness Area within the Gila National Forest, occurred forty years before the Wilderness Act protected tens of millions of acres of roadless lands across the continent.

Yet by 1927, only three years after it was established, the wolfless, roadless wilderness proved to be too much of a hunters' paradise. One of Leopold's colleagues reported an overabundance of deer in the upper Gila drainage, as many as forty-three per square mile, and a shortage of the forage they depended on. Mountain mahogany and live oak stands were depleted. Junipers were browsed as high as deer could reach. The forest was in jeopardy, and so was the future of the deer. With disproportionately few does and fawns in the population, it was clear that the more vulnerable deer were dying of starvation.[10] In "Pineries and Deer," an article about the process of environmental change, Leopold recognized that the loss of forage would limit the number of deer, but he did not yet understand that the number of deer was a limiting factor for forage. The deer were destroying the life of the mountain they depended on.

It takes ecological awareness to grasp the dynamic interdependence of animals, their predators, their food sources, and other aspects of their habitat. This kind of whole systems thinking Leopold had already applied to his study of the links between grazing, erosion, vegetation, and fire in Southwest landscapes. "Our organic resources are not only in a run-down condition," he wrote in 1923, "but in our climate bear a delicately balanced interrelation to each other. . . . Erosion eats into our hills like a contagion, and floods bring down the loosened soil upon our valleys like a scourge. Water, soil, animals, and plants—the very fabric of prosperity—react to destroy each other and us." That unpublished essay shows that he was also thinking about the responsibility human beings had for the loss of prosperity's fabric: "In my opinion, one cannot round out a real understanding of the situation in the Southwest without likewise considering its moral aspects," he wrote.[11] But the meaning of the light in the dying wolf's eyes had not yet dawned on him.

Leopold exercised his sense of responsibility by initiating alliances between groups that had not previously recognized their common interest. While imposing grazing regulations as a fledgling Forest Supervisor, he convinced ranchers that federal restrictions would, in the long run, benefit their herds and themselves. In his campaign against predators, he formed a coalition between sportsmen and stockmen. And in his efforts to have forests managed to grow wildlife as well as trees, he argued that foresters and hunters, as well as loggers, were natural allies. After he moved to Wisconsin in 1924, Leopold formed a game cooperative between a group of hunters from Madison and a group of farmers, with the hunters helping the farmers maintain habitat for wildlife while working with them to protect their land from poachers. Leopold saw beyond the familiar divides in US history between farmers and ranchers, public and private landholders, city residents and country folks. His political map revealed a landscape where everyone stands on—and helps to strengthen—the common ground. This ecological politics represents every interest group, whether people recognize their common interests or not. Leopold was well aware of the clash between exploitation of resources for economic gain and the need for conservation, but he understood the foundation on which all prosperity ultimately rests. "We fancy that industry supports us," he wrote, "forgetting what supports industry."[12]

The art of "thinking like a mountain" that Leopold practiced in developing his ecological understanding of nature, and of people in relation to each other and to the land, does not come naturally to scriptwriters. Our craft relies on dramatic structure to hold an audience, and conflict is the heart of drama. "Where is the conflict?" we asked ourselves in planning the film. Seen within a wide frame of reference, Leopold's life dramatizes a struggle that he was among the first to perceive: the conflict between those whose activities destroy the natural world and those who protect and restore it. The film conveys this throughout, from Leopold's lament regarding the loss of his boyhood landscape ("Man always kills the thing he loves"), to the destruction of soil that filled the skies of the Dust Bowl and the ravages of World War II upon lands and lives on a global scale.

More fundamental than conflict is contrast. The contrast that makes Leopold a contemporary role model is the ability to change that he showed throughout his life. After advocating the killing of varmints, he came to understand the interdependency of predators, prey, and the health of their habitat. Leopold arrived at this realization independently through his process of experimentation, observation, and evaluation. The new science of ecology gave him a theoretical framework to work within. As a scientist, Leopold had the courage to be wrong; he put assumptions to the test and, when proven wrong, changed his views.

A keystone concept in Leopold's "thinking like a mountain" was community. He made comparisons and connections between human and land communities, as when he wrote, "Industries wince with pain when fixers and planners lay violent hands on their highly organized economic community, yet these same industries fix their forests to death with never a flicker of recognition that the same principle is involved. . . . Communities are like clocks, they tick best while possessed of all their cogs and wheels."[13] Leopold looked at the role of human beings within the energy cycle that ranges from microorganisms and plants to top predators and organic decay. But the full implication of the concept of community when applied to people as well as to the greater community of the natural world, the realization that gave the land ethic its basis in experience, which he conveyed through the image of a "fierce green fire," did not come home to him until he traveled in the Sierra Madre range in northern Mexico, across the border from Arizona mountains he knew well.

There, Leopold encountered for the first time land undisturbed by the march of civilization. Apache Indians had hunted in the Gavilan River basin not long before Leopold went there. The Mexican Revolution and its turbulent aftermath prevented the government of Mexico from intervening in that region and its non-Indian population from exploiting its resources. There was an abundance of predators and their prey and a great diversity of species throughout the food chain. Fire was still an active agent of disturbance and renewal. The soils were rich, the forests thriving. In nine days of hunting with bow and arrow, Leopold saw 187 deer but no sign of overgrazing. Trout crowded the streams, and flocks of a pigeon-sized parrot, the *guacamaja*, squawked across the skies. The vitality of this country contrasted strikingly with the condition of the same landscape north of the border. It was there that Leopold "first clearly realized that land is an organism, that all my life I had seen only sick land, whereas here was a biota still in perfect aboriginal health."[14]

The drama of this realization, a pivotal moment in Leopold's life, gives the film its turning point. With the health of the land as his lodestar, Leopold laid the foundations for the fields of wildlife management, conservation biology, and ecosystem restoration. He defined land health as "the capacity for self-renewal in the soils, waters, plants and animals that collectively comprise the land."[15]

Self-renewal, then, is the key to land health. Often disturbance stimulates renewal. One sees this in the wake of a forest fire, a volcanic eruption, and other so-called "natural disasters." Seeds germinate, wildlife returns, landscapes transform themselves. Instead of a vicious cycle that occurs when, for example, a top predator, whether a wolf or a shark, is stripped from an ecosystem, a virtuous cycle spun by the resilience of its members or the regrowth of native species can restore the land's vitality.

The concept of healthy land helped Leopold understand what he had glimpsed in the eyes of the dying wolf. He and she were members of the same community, participants alike in the life of the mountain. That insight led to the idea he would call "the land ethic." As Leopold wrote in *A Sand County Almanac*, "All ethics so far evolved rest upon a single premise: that the individual is a member of a community of interdependent parts. His instincts prompt him to compete for his place in that community, but his ethics prompt him also to cooperate (perhaps in order that there might be a place to compete for). The land ethic simply enlarges the boundaries of the community to include soils, waters, plants and animals, or collectively, the land."[16]

Leopold's idea that human beings are members of the community of life with an ethical responsibility to that entire community is not new at all. Members of hunter-gatherer tribes express this understanding in their myths and prayers and in such practices as thanking animals they kill. That indigenous ethos reaches back into prehistoric times. It grows from the understanding that people who hunt, fish, and gather wild plants have of interdependence with the life around them. Still, Leopold's land ethic was a breakthrough for western civilization, and coming from a scientist, it rang true with a new kind of authority.

The land ethic is not an abstract theory; it puts everyone who understands it to the test. For if we belong to the community of life and if its health requires the capacity for self-renewal among members of that community, then the wellbeing of the world depends on our own ability to undergo a process of self-renewal. That is true on all scales, from civilization as a whole down to individual lives. If Leopold's life story could serve as a model of facing one's errors, relating consciously to the biotic community and learning to act accordingly, a film about him, if successful, would make a valuable contribution.

The film's theme unifies the life with the legacy: how Leopold arrived at the idea of the land ethic and how it is applied today. One problem was to connect the story of Leopold shooting the wolf with the thematic idea. It is one thing to express this on the page, quite another to do so within a few seconds, accompanied by images, in a movie. The solution was to make the transition with a metaphor. "For Leopold," says Curt Meine, "the encounter with the wolf was a fateful turning point on his trail. He followed it until it led to the land ethic." Once that connection is made, "green fire" becomes the metaphor that best symbolizes contemporary manifestations of the land ethic. Speaking of the more than a million organizations in the United States alone that "are working on some aspect of conservation and restoration of the environment," Susan Flader calls this "a veritable 'green fire.' That, I think," she says, "is Aldo Leopold's living legacy."

The film invites the public to bring that legacy into their lives. Leopold once said, "Nothing so important as an ethic is ever written. It evolves in the minds of a thinking community." Curt Meine, speaking at the Yale School of Forestry and Environmental Studies (Leopold's alma mater), tells his audience that this statement is a "stroke of genius, because with that, he liberates the idea, he opens it to the larger thinking community—us." Do we who see the film belong, as did the people in Meine's audience, to a thinking community? Have we found ways of using the land we live on, the waters we depend on, and the air we breathe without spoiling them? *Green Fire* can move us to answer these questions.[17]

UPSTREAM, DOWNSTREAM

In the fall of 1978, a federal SWAT team riding jet boats fought American Indian gillnetters on the Klamath River. This visually compelling event embodied the historic conflict between native people struggling to preserve their ways of life and non-Indians who sought to dominate them.

At the time, few independent filmmakers were making documentaries. Although the first portable, handheld video camera was invented in 1967, access to video editing facilities was limited. Editing film with a razorblade on a flatbed cost little, but film itself was expensive and the cameras cumbersome. Visual documentation of a conflict that became known as the "Salmon War" came from television news crews, newspaper photographers, and people living on the river who shot stills.[1]

Inquiring minds wanted more than the day's news. This was the heyday of investigative journalism. Woodward and Bernstein's reporting on Watergate and its historic result, the resignation of President Nixon, inspired many writers during that era. The founding of the Center for Investigative Reporting in 1977 was a sign of the times. So when newspapers echoed the official explanation for the campaign against gillnetting, that the government was protecting salmon from the Indians, it seemed clear that a more comprehensive and comprehending view was needed. But what was really at stake? How does one understand a fish war?

"Many historical events, hitherto explained solely in terms of human enterprise," wrote Aldo Leopold, "were actually biotic interactions between people and land."[2] For Leopold, "land" was an inclusive term that included wildlife and waters. This was a story involving the relationship between people and salmon as well as between groups of people warring over their relationships with each other. Having been introduced to "Fishermen Along a Salmon River" by Erik H. Erikson and wanting to know every player in this drama, I drove to the Klamath.

Gary Rankle stood on the north bank of the estuary in sight of the bridge that carries Highway 101 across the Klamath River. A US Fish and Wildlife Service biologist, Rankle monitored the gillnetters' catch.

The Indian fishery, he explained, pulled in less than 5 percent of the salmon harvest. Offshore, trollers took 88 percent of the Klamath River salmon catch. Rankle's research directly contradicted his agency's rationale for its assault on Indian fishers—to protect the fall chinook from overfishing. Why then did Fish and Wildlife enforcement agents attack and arrest gillnetters? Why had the federal government established a Court of Indian Offenses to prosecute them? And what were the real reasons for the decline of wild salmon?

Looking beneath the surface of events requires the depth perspective that history provides. It's not only the clash between Indians and non-Indians over salmon that has a history; so does the relationship between people and salmon.

Salmon populated the Pacific Northwest before people did, arriving as the retreating glaciers of the last Ice Age exposed the land surface and carved out waterways. Along great salmon-producing rivers—the Columbia and the Snake, the Klamath and the Trinity—humans settled, enjoying an abundant food that came in the cycle of seasons.

Unlike the goldseekers and settlers who traveled to their country in the mid-nineteenth century, the Klamath River tribes—the Yurok, Hupa, Karuk, and Shasta—evolved a system of economics rooted in the ecology of their riverine homeland. Their traditional technology for catching salmon in temporarily erected weirs allowed large numbers of fish to reach the people upstream and to spawn in abundance, providing salmon for future years.

The tribes developed a shared ceremonial cycle. The timing of the White Deerskin Dance and the Jump Dance coincides with the height of salmon runs. Before the decline of salmon populations in the twentieth century, there were plenty of fish to feed intertribal multitudes at the sacred sites along the riverbanks.

In this relationship between people and salmon, economic, ecological, social, and spiritual needs were intertwined. Ritualization exemplified the understanding from an indigenous perspective of humanity's kinship and interdependence with all forms of life. Regalia worn by dancers in Klamath and Trinity River ceremonies symbolize relationships with other creatures: hides of albino deer, wolf fur headbands, eagle-feathered staffs, headdresses adorned with woodpecker plumage. These relationships are also expressed in prayer. "The prayer is for all the critters, all the deer to come back, to feed all the people. For all the birds to come back, all the salmon to fill the rivers up," said Ike Hillman, who served as priest for the ceremonies when he was fourteen. "When you're out there praying, you're not just praying for yourself or your family. You're praying for everybody on this Earth."

Alfred L. Kroeber called this religion "world renewal." Its motive, he wrote, "is to renew or maintain the established world." In the Karuk language, the name is *pikiawish*: fixing the world. According to Ike's father, Leaf Hillman, *pikiawish* not only restores relationships between people and other forms of life. "It's a time when people are supposed to get rid of your hard feelings toward people. You get in and you get involved and you dance with that person side by side and you get rid of your hard feelings." Kroeber observed this: "The performances are always conducted by competing parties," he wrote. "These match and outdo each other."[3]

The techniques of the Klamath River tribes for ritualizing conflict and fixing the world proved futile in the nineteenth century when people from other lands invaded their country.

During the Gold Rush, there were many battles along the Klamath between miners, vigilante groups, and US military on the one side and tribal members on the other. A "War of Extermination," launched from the town of Yreka, California, and extending across the Siskiyou Mountains into Oregon, destroyed the Shasta tribe, whose only survivors were women who cohabited with miners.[4] The miners' quest for fortune was the Karuks' misfortune. Invaders attacked their villages and killed many people, while others escaped into the mountains. The rugged terrain of the high country gave refuge for families and guerrilla fighters.

Geology as well as geography favored the Klamath River Indians who lived downstream between the confluence with the Trinity River and the estuary. There was little gold in Yurok country. And because a shifting sandbar blocks the river mouth while fog often obscures it completely, forty-niners did not enter the river from the Pacific. Instead, many began an overland trek for gold at the town on Humboldt Bay that is optimistically named Eureka. As a result, Yuroks managed to remain in some of the village sites they had inhabited for hundreds, if not thousands, of years.

From the 1880s into the 1920s, salmon canneries at the mouth of the Klamath employed Indians. They used gillnets instead of weirs to catch fish in the river. The record catch, in 1912, was 17,000 salmon in a day. When Copco, the first hydroelectric dam, was erected across the riverbed in 1918, the runs, especially of spring chinook, which spawned in the Upper Basin, crashed. By the end of the 1920s, there were no canneries. California's response to the decline in salmon populations was to ban the Indian fishery in 1933. Forty years later, after a Supreme Court decision restored Indian fishing rights, commercial and sports fishers blamed the Indians for the decline of fall chinook salmon. Five years after that, the US Fish and Wildlife Service declared a moratorium on Indian fishing and put jetboats on the Klamath to arrest Indians who defied them by "protest fishing." History was repeating itself.

When, in 1978, I came to the Klamath River wanting to understand this conflict, I was not yet a documentary filmmaker. I had written a series of articles for Pacific News Service about the Wounded Knee Occupation and Siege, and I had written a play based on oral history interviews and documentary sources about the Modoc War, which was waged in the 1870s in the Upper Klamath Basin.[5] On this trip, not knowing what my research would lead to, I came equipped with nothing but pen and paper.

In Crescent City, north of the Klamath estuary and south of the Oregon border, Bob Weir, the District Attorney for Del Norte County, complained about Raymond Mattz, whose arrest for gillnetting led to the Supreme Court ruling that reaffirmed Indian fishing rights. Salmon that Mattz and other gillnetters caught are smuggled across the border for sale in Oregon, Weir said, adding that their business had increased in recent years in spite of the fact that the sale of salmon from California rivers was illegal. In 1977, a quarter-million pounds of Klamath River salmon were sold in Oregon. That year, the Bureau of Indian Affairs published regulations to control the Indian fishery, but they went unenforced. And now, he said, the Fish and Wildlife Service operation to enforce a moratorium against gillnetting was being undermined: the US attorney in San Francisco refused to prosecute felony cases against the gillnetters that the newly established Court of Indian Offenses processed. Weir thought California should be in charge. "It's stupid to regulate a fishery from 3,000 miles away. Luckily, no one's been killed—no one that we know of. Nobody's dead except a lot of fish."

Weir explained why he thought it was necessary to target the Indian fishery in response to the decline of salmon populations. "We can't stop logging," he said. "Sportsfishing could be stopped, but their take is only five to eight thousand fish a year, and they benefit the area economically." The secretary of commerce, he added, refuses to curtail ocean commercial fishing. That left Indian gillnetting in his crosshairs, despite the Supreme Court ruling that it was legal.

Raymond Mattz seemed a likely protagonist for this story. In any case, I needed to understand his point of view. Walking the driveway down to his parents' two-story home in Requa, California, on the north bank of the estuary, I passed the redwood plank house with an oval door that the family had inhabited for centuries.[6] At the time, there were plainclothes federal agents in the area, some of them staying a few miles north at the Trees of Mystery motel across the highway from a giant statue of Paul Bunyan and his ox, Babe. Nonetheless, Geneva

Mattz, a tiny woman with a round, wrinkled face, opened the door and invited me in.

Her husband Emery stood by the window watching the river through a telescope. Raymond's twin brother Marvin sat nearby watching television. Diane Bowers, a daughter of their sister Lavina, got me a cup of coffee. She was no taller than her grandmother. Marvin, asking for a refill, called her "Mouse."

Geneva showed me her collection of baskets, dance outfits, feathers, net stones, and jewelry, including dentalium shells, the traditional Yurok money, all adorning a wall in the living room. Hanging among them was a nightstick. It was black, made of plastic with lead inside, about two feet long. I asked her what it was doing there.

Geneva told me that she had plucked it out of the river when she and Lavina were "protest fishing"—demonstrating their right to fish in the face of the federal enforcement operation. She recounted their experience:

> We did it in the day. There were no fish. They were upriver. I wore my Indian gear: my burden basket, my Indian cap, my Indian beads; and we went out and set our net and we sat there and waited.
>
> Then the birds came in. Pelicans were in the lead, then the seagulls, then the shads, and other birds mixed together. They just went around and around above our boat.
>
> In our Indian way, it was something great to the person in the water: a protection, a sign nothing was going to happen to me, that I belong to the land and they know it. I was born and raised here.
>
> Then three boats came of agents geared with clubs and pistols. I prayed. My daughter talked to the feds and told them why we were out here. Then I sang an Indian song to the feds. They said, "Let's get out of here!" One woman agent cut our net first. As she did so, she dropped her club.

Photos taken by Diane Mattz, Raymond's wife, documented this confrontation.

Shortly after Geneva and Lavina refused to submit to the armed agents' demands, the Fish and Wildlife enforcement operation ended. The spiraling of the birds in concert with an elder's prayer song made it appear that Geneva had summoned the spirit of the river to defend the Yurok way of life.[7]

But it was not spirit power that explained the federal withdrawal. The salmon run had ended, and they had bigger fish to fry. There was a power vacuum on the river. The State of California had governed the Klamath River through most of the twentieth century, maintaining that the nineteenth-century Yurok reservation had been liquidated. But once the Supreme Court ruling affirmed that it was still Yurok country and that Indians had fishing rights there, the Carter administration, through the Bureau of Indian Affairs (BIA) as well as the Fish and Wildlife Service, decided to take control.

Yuroks had no federally recognized leadership. Potentially, the BIA could set up an amenable tribal council. But as long as local Indians lived off the bounty of nature, the BIA could not manage the tribe by employing members of cooperative families, as occurred on Indian reservations throughout the country, and leaving the rest in poverty or in jail. Adding to the complexity of the situation was the fact that the Yurok stretch of the Klamath River had been administered as an extension of the Hoopa Valley Indian Reservation, and Yuroks were engaged in a long-running legal battle to receive a share of the reservation's timber revenues. But now it was not clear who would be recognized officially as a Yurok, who would govern their tribe, and who would receive the Hoopa Valley revenues: individual Yuroks or the new tribal government.

Nature abhors a vacuum and so does power. Shortly after the hostilities on the river ended, the assistant secretary of Indian affairs announced, "It is necessary for the Department of Interior through my office to assume complete management of the Reservation assets on behalf of both tribes."[8]

On the day of this decree, Yuroks and Hupas streamed into the chambers of the Hoopa Valley Tribal Business Council to discuss the new situation. "They've got the upper hand," said a councilman about "the feds." "They can do anything they damn please." "That doesn't mean you're going to lay down," shouted a woman from the floor. "They're going to start a war here," said Joyce Croy. "It's time to fight for what is rightfully ours!"

In the lobby outside the council chambers, a television crew from the Soviet Union was conducting interviews; no other media were present except for myself. A man named Igor asked Joyce Croy about her tribe's dependence on subsistence fishing, and he asked someone else about US violations of American Indians' human rights. This was a timely question. President Jimmy Carter had repeatedly accused the Soviets of human rights violations. The Russians could turn the tide of propaganda by showing forcible imposition of neocolonial rule by the Carter administration over American Indian tribes.

Anticipating an invasion of Hoopa Valley, people gathered at Joyce Croy's house to plan their resistance. But the attack did not come. Perhaps the presence of Soviet media deterred it, or the militant response of tribal members.

A larger-scale fishery enforcement operation that had been planned for the following year was canceled. In the mid-eighties, an act of Congress established a new Yurok reservation, along with a process for determining its membership and for developing a tribal government. That government promptly hired fishery biologists to gather data about the river and its wildlife and to manage their habitat. A new chapter in the relationship between people and fish on the Klamath River had begun.

This story deserved, to my mind, to be part of history. But as the news broadcasts vanished from memory and the newspapers yellowed, it appeared that "the Salmon War" would be forgotten. I knew that the articles I had written about it and my play *Watershed*, which had a couple of productions, could not rescue that event from oblivion.

So in 2000, I decided to make a documentary about the fish war. Carlos Bolado, a Mexican director, joined the project. Jack Kohler, the Yurok/Karuk actor who played the part of Rick, modeled on Raymond Mattz, in *Watershed*, had been in films; now he wanted to make them. Having trained in engineering at Stanford and having worked as a contractor, Jack was technically adept. He quickly learned the various tasks of filmmaking.

Carlos and I drove to the mouth of the Klamath to research the movie. We did some interviews, looked for documentary resources, and visited locations on and along the river. We found no one at the Fish and Wildlife Service who was willing to speak about the enforcement operation. I asked to see photographs, correspondence, and other records from 1978. Everything was destroyed, I was told, when the local office of the agency moved to another building.

I expected that Raymond Mattz would be an important character for the film both as a leader of the gillnetters and as the defendant whose case restored their fishing rights. However, he was drinking when Carlos and I visited him. As Carlos videotaped my attempt at an interview, Raymond mumbled and looked down at the ground.

Interviews with other Yuroks went well, but it seemed unlikely we could make the film I had in mind. There was insufficient documentary evidence, no one on the government side of the conflict would speak to us, and the protagonist would not face the camera. We had received preproduction money for a movie with little prospect for success. Instead of being able to have the best possible representation of the opposing sides in the fish war, there was no one who could authoritatively represent either side.

Then came 2001 and another eruption in the volatile history of the Klamath Basin.

Documentary screenwriters find it quite different to work with stories that are fully realized, having happened in the past, than with stories that are ongoing and indeterminate. A film that tells of an event, a life, a work of art, or another complete subject can be scripted in advance. People who might speak about it on camera can be found through publications, conferences, professions, and organizations related to whomever or whatever the film is about. One can collect the documentary resources such as photos and archival film that are available. And one can simply go to the place where the story transpired and ask around. All of the significant incidents are known and can be arranged into a storyline. I had expected to make a film of that kind. But all of a sudden, the hotspot of Klamath River history shifted upriver. Water, not salmon, was at issue, and farmers instead of gillnetters were defending their way of life. This new outbreak encompassed the entire Klamath Basin, bringing farmers and ranchers as well as Indians, other fishers, and federal agencies into the picture. Not only had the temporal frame of reference moved from a definite past to an unknowable future; the spatial frame expanded by more than ten thousand square miles from the estuary to the headwaters. The subject expanded as well. For while the conflict this time involved salmon once again, at its core was the substance on which all life depends.

Water unites the Klamath Basin. Since no road follows the entire course of the river, travel between the mouth and the headwaters takes a long time. Even if people in its scattered communities were so inclined, it would be difficult for them to know each other. But the differences between the tribal members, who comprise the region's largest minority, and the non-Indian population, together with the distance between the downriver fisheries and the upriver forests, farms, and ranches, made it hard for these communities to understand, much less empathize with, each other when a crisis affecting everyone struck the basin. Their disconnectedness gave the documentary project a new purpose. It could represent these diverse populations to each other, as well as to the public at large.

In this situation, impartiality was crucial. Members of the Mattz family had become my friends. Nonetheless, as a reporter, I developed respectful relationships with their adversaries during the fish war, and now federal agencies that had opposed Yurok self-government, along with commercial fishers who were the Indians' rivals in the fight for fish, became their allies in demanding water for endangered wild salmon. Now, regardless of my personal love of salmon and my downriver friendships, I needed to understand the farmers' feelings, their history on the land, and their views in the dispute over the waters of the Klamath Basin.

The differences and distances between the various stakeholders in the Klamath Basin posed an artistic problem along with the personal challenge of transcending their bitter divisions and the geographic challenge of visiting their far-flung communities. What unifying character or theme could hold this emerging picture together?

The immediate task at hand was to follow the story. In 2001, as in 1978, the Klamath Basin suffered from a severe drought. In both years, a consequence was a crash in salmon populations. Only this time, farmers as well as fishers felt the impact. Biological opinions issued by the US Fish and Wildlife Service led a US district court judge to conclude that the Bureau of Reclamation had violated the Endangered Species Act (ESA) in providing water for Klamath Project irrigation: the Bureau had failed to consult with other federal agencies about the water needs of listed species. As a result, on 6 April 2001, shortly before the growing season began, the Bureau announced that Klamath Project farmers would receive less than an eighth of the water for their crops than they counted on.

In this crisis, the farmers' adversary, like the gillnetters' a generation earlier, was the federal government. And like the gillnetters, the farmers responded with civil disobedience. They felt betrayed by a government that had removed Indians from their land for settlement during the Modoc War, had drained large lakes to increase their land area in the early twentieth century, had fought the downriver fishing tribes in 1978, but now was siding with the natives against producers of food.

Joining forces with Frontiers of Freedom, patriot militias, and other right-wing organizations that fought environmental laws in general and the Endangered Species Act in particular, ranchers and farmers in the Upper Basin planned a high-profile protest of the water cutoff: a bucket brigade. Filling the streets of Klamath Falls, protestors would take bucketfuls of water from the river, pass them hand to hand along Main Street, and pour them, illegally, into the main irrigation canal.

That was an event my film project could not miss. There was enough left in the preproduction budget to rent a truck, spend a night in a hotel, do a day's shoot, and return the next night. Jack Kohler arranged for us to interview a fisheries biologist and a cultural spokesperson who worked for the Klamath Tribes. Tribal representatives had refused interviews by national media, fearing that publicity in conjunction with the bucket brigade would inflame antagonism between non-Indians and tribal members. The documentary gave them an opportunity to present their views in a larger context at a less fervent time. I arranged to interview John Crawford, who had been quoted in a news article about the rally. He, I thought, could represent a farmer's point of view in the documentary.

On 7 May 2001, when we reached Klamath Falls after an early-morning shoot on the reservation, thousands of people crowded Veterans Park as a parade of speakers addressed them from a podium. Some waved signs that said "A Future of Desperation," "Klamath Farmers Are Endangered Species," and "Water for People, not Fish"—as if no one's livelihood depended on fish. When John Crawford spoke, he was eloquent: "I stand before you today humbled by the magnitude of your presence and humbled to be present in your hearts." He was sympathetic: "For two months I have had a huge hole in the pit of my stomach. It's like the void created by the loss of a loved one." And he was angry: "It's time to treat those who bring this horrible irreparable harm to this basin and our lives accordingly."

After the rally, our cameras, along with media crews for broadcast and cable news stations, captured the scene of buckets of water, each stamped with the slogan "Amend the ESA," passed from one person to the next for a mile along Main Street, then carried uphill to a bridge where, ceremoniously, before a cheering crowd, each bucketful was poured into the irrigation canal below. Then, as arranged, I met John Crawford and brought him to the high school stadium where my colleagues had set up for the interview.

With a Mexican directing the camera and an American Indian doing sound, Crawford seemed a different person from the man at the podium. He spoke of fishing and of his "ties to the Native American people at the mouth of the Klamath. The best man at my wedding was a Yurok Indian." That was interesting. Like native people, ranchers and farmers love the outdoors. In this regard, cowboys and Indians have more in common than either group has with many urbanites. "Our farms are family farms," Crawford told us, "and it is completely unfair that our farms should lose all of their water because of endangered species. People are leaving farms their people have had for generations. This is the end of a way of life."

Crawford could have offered the film more than a character representing the views of his community. Had there been time to win his trust and enough resources to continue the production trip past that day, we might have gone to his farm, seen his life on the land, and come to know him.

His sound bite was valuable nonetheless, for Crawford's words and that day's demonstration expressed the distress of Klamath Project farmers. Unable to grow crops, many had to rely on food assistance.

That summer, patriot militias from Montana, Nevada, Washington, and Idaho rallied to their support. Believers in a nation ruled by white Christian men under God, militia members considered the United

States government a tyranny that had to be overthrown. Members of the Jarbidge Shovel Brigade in Elko, Nevada, who had dug open a road the Forest Service closed to protect a canyon the year before, forged two ten-foot-tall buckets. One was placed on Main Street, a prominent memorial of the bucket brigade. The other giant bucket toured the country atop a flatbed trailer, collecting money, food, and supplies for the farmers.

Allied with the patriot militias, local farmers went beyond symbolic protest. Secretly at night, activists broke into the Klamath Project head gates and, using saws and blowtorches, opened the main valve that releases water into the "A" Canal. Although this was a violation of federal law, the sheriff proclaimed that he would not press charges.

On Independence Day the revolt went public. About a hundred flag-waving protesters marched to the head gates and turned the wheel that let the water flow. According to Jeff Head, an Idaho resident who took part in this display of patriot activism, when US Marshals arrived, "the farmers and their supporters" began singing hymns to them. On his website, "The Stand at Klamath Falls," Head wrote that the Marshals "stopped cold as if running into a barrier and backed up to their car. Several of these faithful farmers believe that God in Heaven took a hand in their behalf that day." Here was the right-wing equivalent of the belief that the spirit of the river, expressed by birds spiraling above Geneva's boat, intervened on behalf of the gillnetters, making Fish and Wildlife agents abandon their operation twenty-three years earlier. In each story, federal forces yielded to a higher power.

The water cutoff in the Upper Basin, which put those who fished in the rivers and in the ocean at odds with the farming community, gained significance as a scene within the national political drama. Less than a year after the contested Bush vs. Gore presidential election, the Klamath Basin, like the nation, was split into red and blue zones. Coastal California was blue; the headwaters across the Oregon/California border were crimson. President Bush had narrowly lost Oregon's electoral votes in 2000; the US Senate was evenly divided; and Oregon's Republican senator, Gordon Smith, was running for reelection in 2002. The farmers' hostility to the federal government for halting irrigation had become a political liability. During the summer of militant civil disobedience, the Bush administration decided to release water for the next growing season regardless of the needs of fish.

With the farmers' plight commanding national attention, the tribes wanted to make their perspective known. Soon our documentary film crew was shooting Karuk dipnetting and Yurok gillnetting and interviewing tribal elders as well as fishers, biologists, and political leaders.

Having Jack Kohler on the project helped the movie gain access to people and places in Indian country. Jack himself was raised in San Francisco, and although he had played American Indian leaders from Crazy Horse to Tecumseh on stage and screen, he lacked firsthand experience with tribal ways of life. When Leaf Hillman invited him to take part in a *pikiawish* ceremony at the sacred dance grounds near Ishi Pishi Falls, Jack nervously agreed to do so.

It became clear that traveling through the country of his ancestors and meeting contemporaries who lived traditionally as best they could had a profound effect on Jack. Being Yurok/Karuk on his father's side, Jack was discovering his roots along the Klamath River. Being a Welshman on his mother's side and a Stanford graduate, Jack related well to members of non-Indian communities. I realized that his journey could give our work-in-progress the unifying storyline it needed. Going from the mouth of the river to the headwaters as the on-camera narrator, Jack could recount the dramatic history of people and salmon from indigenous times to the Klamath bucket brigade. As he traveled, Jack could seek to understand all sides of the Klamath Basin conflict. Our idea was that although Jack is, and looks like, an American Indian, he could bridge the ethnic, economic, and political divide that was driving events from one calamity to the next.

The basin's crisis shifted focus from water back to fish in 2002. The dewatering of the Klamath to serve irrigation and political interests led to the unprecedented die-off of tens of thousands of salmon that September. As fish floated on the river, clustering several deep in the eddies and washing up on the shore, birds swarmed, pecking at their carcasses. "I literally watched grown men cry," said Lyle Marshall, chairman of the Hoopa Valley Tribal Business Council. "Stand on the river bank and cry. Not over a dead salmon, but over such a catastrophic injury to our world."

This was a disaster not only for tribal members but also for sports fishers and for the commercial salmon fishery several years later. Not only did spawners die in the estuary, countless thousands of juvenile fish died in the river that year, never reaching the ocean. Those fish, on reaching maturity, would have returned to the Pacific coast three to five years later. Predictably, in 2005, the lack of Klamath River salmon shut down the offshore salmon fishing industry along seven hundred miles of the West Coast.

Mass media, as well as fishers and environmentalists, blamed farmers of the Klamath Project and the politicians who catered to them for the crash in salmon populations. Our documentary, *River of Renewal*, had a wider lens. More than half of the water from the main tributary, the Trinity, was blocked at Trinity Dam. Its flow was reversed and diverted in 2002, as in previous years, to generate electricity for urban power in Sacramento and to irrigate crops in California's Central Valley. Referring to the canals of the Central Valley Project, Lyle Marshall said "the cement river" took water that would otherwise have flowed into the Klamath out of the basin altogether. A return trip to the upper basin enabled the production to show what family farmers had undergone, while being blamed for the die-off, as giant agribusinesses to the south used Klamath River water to produce crops on their lands. "We were raising mint at that time," said John Anderson. "And we weren't able to put water on our mint. We ultimately had 100 percent loss on our mint." Cattle "kind of kept us alive that year."

By mid-decade residents throughout the Klamath Basin knew that every community had suffered from the decline of salmon. Events had taken an unexpected turn: the tribes that had been aided by the Endangered Species Act were victims once again, their fisheries stricken by shallow waters, while yesterday's heroes, the farmers, were villainized. Cutting through this melodrama was compassion. Farmers who received disaster relief funds from coastal residents in 2001 sent aid to commercial fishing families who lost their livelihoods years later. Geographic isolation combined with political polarization gave way to a sense of tragedy, the recognition that people fighting for what they felt was right had victimized themselves as well as others. Many realized that unless things took a new turn, their shared fate would be years of fruitless conflict, with court decisions and political calculations instead of the needs of the basin and its communities determining outcomes. People who loved the outdoors, who loved being on the land and on the waters, would remain locked in bitter dispute for the rest of their lives.

If the essence of drama is conflict, this story had plenty. One rival documentary bore the title *Upstream Battle*; another was called *Battle for the Klamath*. But for a writer who had observed events on the Klamath for decades, the most dramatic contrast was between the history of conflict in that region and the work toward reconciliation that came in the wake of the salmon die-off and its ripple effects. That contrast gave *River of Renewal* its central story.

At a Watershed Conference at the Oregon Institute of Technology in 2004, Mike Connelly, a rancher and executive director of the Klamath Basin Ecosystem Foundation, declared that people had to change the ways they spoke to each other. Connelly wanted something new: a forum in which people from the divided basin communities became able to say what was in their hearts. To this end, he and fellow organizer Alice Kilham, who worked for the Bureau of Reclamation, asked Bob

Chadwick, a former forest supervisor of the Winema National Forest, to demonstrate methods of conflict resolution and consensus building.

In the year and a half that followed, Chadwick led five stakeholders' workshops, each in a different region within the Klamath Basin. Participants were asked to share their fears about what might happen to the basin as well as their hopes about what could happen. Everyone had the opportunity to speak without interruption, and after someone spoke, a designated listener repeated the main points so that speakers could be sure they were heard before the discussion moved on. This time-consuming process ensured that people got beyond knee-jerk responses. It revealed conviction, experience, and knowledge behind views different from one's own. And it exposed common ground. People from all of the communities in the Klamath Basin realized that while they were fighting each other, outside interests were extracting profits from the river system without benefiting the regional economy. Their attention turned to the four hydroelectric dams on the Klamath that disrupt the river's flow, heat the water in stagnant reservoirs, and block salmon from hundreds of miles of spawning habitat, perpetuating conditions that harm the region ecologically as well as economically. Learning to work together in these meetings, participants developed a shared vision of a future for the Klamath Basin that would preserve everyone's way of life.[9]

Among those who took the risk of reconciliation were Troy Fletcher, a fishery biologist and former executive director of the Yurok Tribe, and Greg Addington, who headed an upper basin farmers' association. In 2005, Fletcher, who had repeatedly denounced "the irrigators," proposed that farmers and tribal members stop using the media to attack each other. Addington and other leaders of the farm community agreed, and the adversaries tried to understand what they had in common. "Instead of fighting each other," Fletcher explained, "We went out for beers." Some farmers were outraged. "My friends," said Addington, "are my enemies, and my enemies are my friends."[10]

Following the Chadwick sessions, a series of meetings took place that led to the Klamath Basin Restoration Agreement. The KBRA was negotiated by representatives of twenty-six stakeholders, including federal, state, and county agencies; the tribes; and irrigation, conservation, and fishing organizations. In doing so, participants created a public space responding to the crisis of their region.

What made these restoration meetings powerful was the recognition that the future of the Klamath Basin was at stake. The hydroelectric dams on the mainstem were up for relicensing by the Federal Energy Regulatory Commission. If they functioned for another fifty years as they had for the last half century, the wild salmon species of the Klamath were likely to perish. That threatened not only the tribes, the sportfishing economy, and the commercial fishing industry, but also the farmers. Farmers dreaded endless lawsuits and water cutoffs as salmon populations declined. And they feared losing the cheap rates for electricity that had been set half a century earlier if the dams were relicensed.

Dams were not the only cause of the decline of salmon. But at this moment in the history of the Klamath, they took center stage. For the movie, that was fortunate, for dams cast a large shadow. In a story about water and salmon, they offered a dramatic image of the contending interests. And the resolution of the issue of dam relicensing offered a last act, a completion of the drama.

When the Klamath River and upper basin tribes along with non-Indian fishers began to campaign for dam removal, a corporation in Scotland owned PacifiCorp, the company that owns and operates the hydroelectric dams. After two years of shareholders' meetings in Edinburgh marred by Indian drumming and unwanted media attention, Scottish Power sold PacifiCorp to Warren Buffett's Berkshire Hathaway. Its shareholders convene in Omaha every year, traveling around the planet to what is called "the Woodstock of Capitalism." In May 2008, executive producer Steve Michelson and I crashed their party, as did dam-removal demonstrators. During the party, people whose wealth had increased thanks to Buffett's portfolio bought jewelry at Florsheim's—one of the many companies owned by Berkshire Hathaway, and they milled, drinks in hand, in a roped-off area of the mall outside that store. Suddenly, women in basket caps and other Klamath River Indians started shouting "Un-dam the Klamath!" as they unfurled a banner demanding that Buffett sign a dam-removal agreement. Michelson videotaped young men falling as if dead in front of the banner. Other demonstrators outlined their bodies with chalk. That protest gave the film's climactic scene exciting footage.

In order to speak to Buffett at the shareholders' meeting, one has to stand in line long before it begins. Members of the Klamath campaign, including Leaf Hillman's son Chook Chook, waited all night beside the 18,000-seat Qwest Center to be among the first to address the legendary chairman. The next morning, when their turn came, Buffett refused to respond directly; a PacifiCorp representative read a prepared statement instead. After a number of speakers brought up the Klamath, Buffett barred that subject from further mention at the meeting.

But Buffett, or actually PacifiCorp, did sign the agreement. In November, days after the election of Barack Obama, PacifiCorp joined the governors of Oregon and California and the Secretary of the Interior as signators of the Klamath Hydropower Settlement Agreement (KHSA). (I announced the signing at the American Indian Film Festival's awards night, having received, with Jack Kohler, a "best documentary" award for *River of Renewal*.) The KHSA, in tandem with the restoration agreement (KBRA), delineated a process of engineering studies and biological research, watershed restoration, and other measures leading to the demolition of all four hydroelectric dams on the Klamath. This would be the largest dam removal and wild river renewal project in US history.

A film, unlike most episodes in the course of human affairs, has a beginning, middle, and end; and these parts are related in ways that create a sense of completeness. In reality, the Klamath controversy remains unresolved. Those tandem agreements came under fire from uncompromising opponents, including environmental organizations, upstream ranchers, and right-wing politicians.

Years later, a third agreement resulted from the process of conflict resolution and consensus building that I witnessed in the Klamath Basin. A decades-long water rights adjudication process in Oregon concluded that the Klamath Tribes had senior water rights and that their use of water to protect aquatic species superseded the rights of farmers and ranchers in the upper basin to irrigate crops and keep pastures green. Soon after this decision was made, drought once again caused a crisis that spurred historic change. The Klamath Tribes' assertion of their right to increase flows into Upper Klamath Lake, which otherwise would have watered private lands, forced ranchers to move their herds or sell them off, and that brought ranchers who had been hostile to tribal members into negotiations with them. The result was the Upper Basin Comprehensive Agreement, which provides irrigation for farmers and ranchers in return for water use reduction measures and wildlife habitat protection. "With the three agreements in place," announced Interior Department Secretary Sally Jewell, "we have the tools needed to restore the basin, advance the recovery of its fisheries, uphold trust responsibilities to the tribes, and sustain our ranching heritage from the headwaters of the Klamath to the ocean."

In striking contrast to the reconciliation that has occurred in a rural region between parties who have historically been adversaries— divided by warfare, differences in race and culture, and economic interests—the polarized and often paralyzed US Congress failed to pass an appropriations bill that would implement their agreements.

In Requa, California, on 6 April 2016, four months after the bill expired, Secretary Jewell, California Governor Jerry Brown, Oregon Governor Kate Brown, and PacifiCorp CEO Stefan Bird signed, on riverside tables Yuroks use for cleaning fish, an agreement to remove the hydroelectric dams on the Klamath. This new dam-removal and river restoration plan bypasses Congress altogether, going instead through the Federal Energy Regulatory Commission. Ironically, it omits the stakeholders' water-sharing measures that were negotiated to benefit farmers and ranchers whose Republican representatives killed the appropriations bill.

Although my film was completed long before the eventual outcome came clearly into view and although more turns in the plot are bound to occur before the removal of the dams, which is planned for 2020, the storyline in *River of Renewal* about the conflict that preceded the original Klamath Hydropower Settlement Agreement has an enduring timeliness.[11]

So does the theme of Jack's journey. Unlike Kunta Kinte of the famous television drama *Roots*, Jack finds more than his ethnic identity in the homeland of his ancestors. He finds his roots "in a tangle of connectedness." That metaphor suggests that water nurtures all, ranchers and Indians, farmers and federal officials, humans and salmon. Historically, the Klamath Basin has been united by water but divided by people. By presenting the controversy over salmon and water as an ecological drama whose protagonists recognize their connectedness and join forces to fix the world, the film furthers reconciliation within that region while telling a story whose roots extend into watersheds far beyond the Klamath.

PART FOUR

THE HUMAN WORLD

*The destiny of the world is determined less by the battles that
are lost and won than by the stories it loves and believes in.*
—Harold Goddard

*We think we tell stories, but stories often tell us, tell
us to love or to hate, to see or to be blind.*
—Rebecca Solnit

▦ IMAGINING FREEDOM

We create our own myths—narratives in which we are hero or victim, agents of destiny or subjects of fate—and we ignore facts that don't fit our favored narratives. Yet acknowledgment of those facts is crucial for awareness and growth. What's more, those facts, due to their incongruity, can be funny.

One way to look beyond family dramas, dreams of glory, or whatever tale has a grip on us is to recognize ourselves in stories others tell. Such moments, which in everyday life open minds, may have comic or tragic effects in literature, and they offer insights for makers of nonfiction works. For Hannah Arendt, the scene in which Odysseus, in Alcinous's palace, listens "to the story of his own deeds and sufferings" and weeps tears of remembrance represents "'reconciliation with reality,' the catharsis, which, according to Aristotle, was the essence of tragedy, and, according to Hegel, was the ultimate purpose of history."[1]

Oedipus's recognition that he killed his father and married his mother comes from the investigation he conducts to discover the cause of a plague that besets his kingdom. As Sophocles' tragedy unfolds, the king gathers clues and interprets them until what he thinks to be the truth collapses under the weight of what he learns. Similarly, documentary filmmakers inform themselves by gathering each valid scrap of evidence and by seeking testimony from every credible witness. Whatever preconceptions they have must meet the test of whatever they find out.

The bits of knowledge investigative storytellers collect are like the pieces in a jigsaw puzzle one assembles to make a picture. A jigsaw puzzle may seem an odd metaphor for the making of a documentary. There is no box the pieces come in, nor any image that displays the assembled picture, and the number of potential pieces is limitless. But as a cinematic analogy, an expanding puzzle with changing parts is apt. The bits of information in themselves do not lead to a synthesis but only to more information that raises more questions and leads to even more facts. At first, the pieces filmmakers pay closest attention to and the new information they acquire depend on their prior understanding of the situation. Whatever conceptual approach or thesis they have will be confirmed, altered, or abandoned and replaced with something else. Reality is not simply "out there" to be documented.

To reach an understanding of one's subject takes imagination. As makers assemble the pieces into a comprehensive and comprehensible pattern, a provisional puzzle-box image comes into view. The picture they envision changes as they fit the pieces together; this is an iterative process. Moreover, they have to figure out what appears in the foreground and what goes in the background. Whether the storytellers favor David or Goliath, they place what is close to them at a sufficient distance to see the characters without bias and bring those who are distant close enough to understand the incidents from their vantage points. "This distancing of some things and bridging the abysses to others," observed Hannah Arendt, "is part of the dialogue of understanding, for whose purposes direct experience establishes too close a contact and mere knowledge erects artificial barriers."[2] Eventually, as filmmakers put all the relevant information into perspective, a vision of the story emerges.

Having fit the pieces together and decided what the story will be, makers set the resulting picture within a frame. The movie gains coherence when they choose a beginning and an end, a unifying action and theme.

Makers of documentaries about historic events have various themes, a wide range of stories, and numerous potential characters to choose from. They also have the task of distinguishing truth from falsehood. For in democracies as well as in dictatorships, repeated lies keep multitudes from recognizing reality; and the most effective lies, like the most enlightening truths, come packaged as stories. Often there is a picture on the puzzle box that the facts do not fit. Indeed, it is the very absence of facts that makes them compelling. As Arendt observed, the art of the totalitarian leader "consists in using, and at the same time, transcending, the elements of reality, of verifiable experiences, in the chosen fiction, and in generalizing them into regions which then are definitely removed from all possible control by individual experience. With such generalizations, totalitarian propaganda establishes a world fit to compete with the real one, whose main handicap is that it is not logical, consistent, and organized."[3]

Nonfiction filmmakers do organize their material, working within limits that are inherent to their medium. Each movie is self-contained. Requiring a viewer's sustained attention, it can last only so long. The length of a movie or the number of shows in a series that will treat one's given subject is a decision filmmakers have to make. One criterion to consider is the available funding; another, the potential audience; a third, the way the work will reach that audience. If the film is to be broadcast on PBS, the "broadcast hour" of fifty-six minutes and forty seconds may define the length of at least one version.

An important criterion is what there is to show of an historical subject as it happened, when it occurred in the present tense; for that immediacy and the uncertainty about the future generates suspense and holds the audience. "This is the realm," wrote Arendt, "where freedom is a worldly reality, tangible in words which can be heard, in deeds which can be seen, and in events which are talked about, remembered, and turned into stories before they are finally incorporated into the great storybook of human history."[4]

To be clear: what Arendt called "the great storybook" is a book *of* stories, not a bible or novel; there is no overarching storyline. History in itself "has no purpose!" says Tom Stoppard's Alexander Herzen in *The Coast of Utopia*, explaining that "history knocks at a thousand gates at every moment, and the gatekeeper is chance."[5] As James Atlas sees it, "History is a series of random events organized in a seemingly sensible order."[6] That order is determined retroactively.

Each story carries its meaning within itself. But that meaning is not inherent in the subject nor is it stated in so many words. If it were merely a message, there would be no point in making a movie. What the film does in telling a story is focus minds on the theme that channels its meaning. Which theme gets emphasized, where the storyteller begins and ends the tale, who the principal characters are, how things turn out—all of these choices contribute to the meaning the story conveys. That meaning is subject to interpretation, evolving, like Aldo Leopold's land ethic, "in the minds of a thinking community."

A case in point is *Freedom on My Mind*, a feature-length documentary produced and directed by Connie Field and Marilyn Mulford about the Mississippi Freedom Summer.[7]

The title announces the movie's theme. A prelude introduces the film's central characters: three African-Americans in Mississippi. The first act reveals conditions of servitude and segregation that make freedom for them, as the song says, "a constant struggle." What they need is freedom *from* those conditions. Freedom as positive possibility for self-realization is inconceivable. "You don't dream things that you can't imagine," says L. C. Dorsey, who chopped cotton on a plantation when she was seven. The straw boss opposed letting children go to school when there was work to be done. Her father accompanied her to the school bus stop holding a rifle. When Curtis Hayes was a boy, he "worked for white folks every day" and kept getting into bloody fights.

His parents tried to teach fear to their angry son. On her eleventh birth-day, when Endesha Ida Mae Holland was babysitting for a white family, the mother summoned the girl upstairs where her husband waited. He pulled Ida Mae "down onto the bed and had intercourse with me." Ida Mae didn't tell her parents. "They'd get killed if they said something about it." But if a black man even looked at a white woman, says L. C. Dorsey, he could be lynched for "eye rape."

Theirs is a classic David vs. Goliath story. Goliath is amply represented. "This is a white man's civilization," a president of the American Psychological Association informs us. "I am a Mississippi segregationist, and I am proud of it," proclaims Governor Ross Barnett. When the civil rights movement pressures the South to integrate schools, lunch counters, and bus stations, we see the violent response of white Mississippians, including beatings, brutal arrests by the police, and murders of black activists.

"It was ordinary people who were challenging all this," says Marshall Ganz, a college student from California who was spending the summer of 1964 in Mississippi. "It was the call."

One person who hears the call is far from ordinary. When Bob Moses of the Student Nonviolent Coordinating Committee comes to Mississippi from New York City and organizes a voting rights campaign, he becomes known, to Curtis Hayes and others, as Martin Luther King's brother.

Like King, Moses has a gift for leadership and that rare combination of physical and moral courage. After Herbert Lee, an activist he worked with, is killed, "We took it upon ourselves," Moses tells us, "to go out nightly searching for people who had witnessed the killing. It was really very scary." He decided that "they will have to kill us to get us out of here." Then three civil rights workers are murdered near Philadelphia, Mississippi, just as college students are training to take part in Freedom Summer. Moses makes it clear to the young men and women from the North that they are free to go home. Understanding "there's a real moral question in terms of involvement of other people," he tells them that if they leave, no one will consider them cowards, and if they stay, he will be right with them, enduring whatever they do. "It was incredibly powerful," says Chicagoan Heather Booth, "and I left that meeting not only knowing that I would be going down to Mississippi, but that this would be the course for the rest of my life." That spirit of determination despite the danger of violence drives the second act of *Freedom on my Mind*.

Like Moses, another SNCC leader, Fannie Lou Hamer, has remarkable charisma. A plantation timekeeper who was fired and evicted on

Time and chance happen to all, as Ecclesiastes says, and that applies especially to documentary filmmaking. What goes into a documentary depends largely on the filmmaker's access to the subject, the time when the film is produced, and the length of time it takes to complete it, which often depends on the availability of funding. Until the editing process is well underway, one can't be sure how the sequences will work together or how the story will end—a crucial question to answer, since the meaning of a story flows from its resolution.

Despite these uncertainties, a documentary screenwriter can write a pre-editing script that conveys a clear and comprehensive vision of the film. While playwrights draw from memory and imagination in writing dialogue, screenwriters have transcripts, with the best lines selected and sorted by subject and speaker, to draw from. The questions about what to cut, what to include, and in which order to arrange the sequences have provisional answers.

One decision that can be made when scripting is how to frame the story: how small or how large that frame should be to contain a picture that is both coherent and illuminating.

For example, in addition to focusing on an exemplary megafire and opening out from there to look at wildfires and forestry in this country in this century, Kevin White and I could make our large subject small by looking at it from a planetary perspective. Megafires are seen from space. The Rim Fire was photographed from a NASA satellite. Metaphorically, the Rim of the World vista point, which gave the fire its name, is Earth's horizon as seen by an astronaut.

A movie about wildfires and forests in the Anthropocene implicitly asks whether humanity's relationship with fire will enter a new phase.[10] The answer can come only in retrospect at some point in the future. The documentary Kevin White and I are producing is but one story in a succession of stories whose subject has driven human evolution; a subject both familiar and strange, creative and destructive, precisely controlled and largely beyond control. As different kinds of fire fuel the technologies that people use, wildfire on the ground and carbon in the atmosphere will continue to eradicate boundaries between the human and natural worlds, transforming lives in ways that stories will reveal in times to come.

 **EPILOGUE**

"Theory" and "theater" have a shared root in the word for contemplation: *theáomai*, which means to observe intently and to grasp the significance of what one sees. All three words stem from the word for sight: *théa*. Documentaries go beyond the theatrical and the theoretical, for they show real actors in real places and events as they happened, as well as witnesses' accounts and explanations.

A place for perception— like Homer's Olympus, from which gods gaze on the human spectacle; or the *mesa* where Calderón saw his patient's troubles; or the twin Keck telescopes on Mauna Kea, eyes of the planet onto the universe—is rarely self-evident. It has to be recognized or created. That is what occurs at the beginning of *The Law in These Parts*, when the filmmakers build the stage on which judges are to sit and be judged against the backdrop of historical footage.

Civilization has a visual emphasis. Much of the power of documentary films comes from the visual evidence it presents. Yet it is the combination of audio and visual sources that makes documentary storytelling convincing. For storytelling is traditionally an aural experience. And many of the best documentaries are found in podcasts and on the radio.

An excellent example of finding a place for perception comes from a radio documentary. Looking for "a story that would probe the human side of the Israeli–Palestinian conflict," Sandy Tolan "encountered many dead ends and broken leads, but then," says Tolan, "I came across something real: the true story of one house and two families who shared a common history." That house east of Tel Aviv, made of Jerusalem stone, is the place where the drama of an Israeli and a Palestinian family plays out both in his radio piece and the book Tolan wrote with the same title: *The Lemon Tree*.[1]

In developing stories that represent their subjects, makers discover the place that gives themselves and then the public a clear and comprehensive vantage point for seeing and hearing.

The place for perception *par excellence* is the Internet, which lets people anywhere access sounds, texts, and images from everywhere, learn more about any topic from a multiplicity of sources, and communicate with others no matter who or where they are or even, as artificial intelligence improves, no matter which languages they speak.

The Internet is changing the ways viewers watch and respond to documentaries, and it is transforming the medium itself. There is an emerging synergy between the entertainment value of storytelling, the horizontal connectivity of web communications, and the vertical depth of digital information resources. Just as the invention of writing and then the printing press and then mass media increased the reach and influence of storytelling, so does the online proliferation of documentaries. Just as the combination of narrative fiction with the technology of moving pictures gave birth to the feature film, so is the fusion of computers, social media, movies, and television generating new modes of reality-based storytelling.

As digital devices shrink in size and become more available around the world, the Internet offers an increasingly valuable and affordable tool for those who would expand public understanding. At the same time, it gains power as a means of surveillance, disinformation, deception, distraction, and indoctrination.

One of the first questions filmmakers ask is, who is the audience? The Internet provides opposite answers: a potentially global public and niche viewers; citizens of the world and private individuals who access only what already interests them. This paradox poses a challenge for documentary makers whose subjects are unappealing or unfamiliar to most people yet need to be widely known. In such cases, it becomes crucial to determine what is meaningful about that subject on the deepest level, to understand it from the most revealing vantage point, and to find the story that best conveys it to the public.

The Internet gives makers an invaluable and multifaceted toolkit as they do this. They can build their audience from the beginning. Early forms of public engagement can include recommendations of characters, information about relevant incidents, and research resources. Filmmakers can post clips from a work in progress and seek explanations, interpretations, and related footage. Social media allow them to bypass the bottlenecks of foundations and governmental funders via crowdsourcing. Through such activities, documentary makers can take into account a multiplicity of views beyond what one hears from colleagues and audiences at work-in-progress screenings.

In making stories that represent reality, the places for seeing are not just physical, such as a mountaintop or the course of a river, or technological, such as an observatory or the Internet. They are political in the broadest sense, for there are countries where independent media are neither made nor viewed, at least not openly. And they are personal, in that it takes character to look beyond one's experiences, prejudices, influences, and interests in creating nonfiction stories. The place of places where impartial seeing becomes possible is the world, that in-between realm that relies on the presence of multiple perspectives. Like a table around which conversations occur, the world we share in common is revealed by true stories.[2]

When contributing to this world, one needs illumination from the clearest lights. Values that, while widely shared, are usually implicit guide nonfiction storytellers. These are values of individual freedom, respecting the ability of people to disclose who they are in public and to be who they are in private; the courage to challenge dominant authorities, powerful ideologies, and conventional wisdom; and faith in reason as expressed through skepticism and the scientific method.

The exercise of these values requires openness to pluralism as opposed to limitation within restrictive identities defined in contrast to and defended against the Other. Tolerance and understanding come from observing dynamic tensions within the psyche and between individuals, within societies and between societies—the stuff of stories. The ability to imagine the Other as oneself and to understand multiple perspectives, which connects the Axial Age with the Anthropocene, safeguards, recreates, and expands the world. Whatever challenges the years to come may bring, that ability, which is potentially if not actually present in every person, gives reason for hope.

▟ Acknowledgments

I am grateful to everyone who read and commented on this book at various stages of its development. In reading the first complete draft and responding with appreciation and criticism, Claire Schoen was especially helpful, and Jonah Most's thoughtful response to an early draft was encouraging. Marianne Keddington-Lang, the editor of my book *River of Renewal, Myth and History in the Klamath Basin*, and Michael Denneny, a friend from graduate school who became a renowned editor at St. Martin's Press, did me the favor of reading *Stories Make the World* and recommending ways to improve it. My friend and filmmaking colleague Steve Dunsky not only read and critiqued a late draft of the manuscript but also proofread it and caught a number of errors. Another dear friend and fellow filmmaker, Justine Shapiro, offered to proofread the copy-edited text and found that she was reading for pleasure.

The other family members, friends, colleagues, and scholars who read drafts of one or more chapters are Nancy Abrams, Christopher Beaver, Alexa Dilworth, Dale Djerassi, Ann Dunsky, Connie Field, Susan L. Flader, Mark Freeman, China Galland, B. Z. Goldberg, Mike Hamilburg, Judy Irving, Bernie Krause, Ruth Landy, Bill Lang, Carol Lashof, Sandra Luft, Malcolm Margolin, Curt Meine, Kate Mendeloff, Steve Michelson, Judith Montell, Rachel Most, Marilyn Mulford, Malcolm North, Emmy Scharlatt, Gerda Schoenfeld, Douglas and Kaye Sharon, William Theodore, Marilyn Vihman, Rebecca Westerfield, Kevin White, and Eve Yalom.

I also thank the actor and playwright Corey Fischer; Sharon Higel, curator of the Fresno Historical Society; Jennifer Kilmer, director of the Washington State Historical Society; David Nicandri, a former Washington State Historical Society director; Jonah Willihnganz, director of the Stanford Storytelling Project; Andy Ross, a book agent and formerly the manager of Cody's, one of the great independent bookstores; and Carl Wikander, who composed this book's index.

It was my good fortune that Berghahn Books, an independent publisher, took a risk on an unconventional manuscript by an unknown author. Working with senior editor Chris Chappell has been a pleasure, and his guidance improved this book considerably.

I have more to thank Claire Schoen for than her reading of the first draft of *Stories Make the World* and for allowing me to use the title of an audio show she produced with Corey Fischer to name this book. When we met, I was writing plays with the Dell'Arte Players Company and she was a documentary filmmaker. Claire introduced me to the community of San Francisco Bay Area media professionals. Her ability to organize far-ranging sources of information and her mastery of the production process helped me apply a dramatist's skills to nonfiction screenwriting. The home we made for and with each other has sustained me in everything I have done ever since.

 SELECTED FILMOGRAPHY: STEPHEN MOST

WILDER THAN WILD, writer/producer
2017—An hour-long documentary about wildfires and climate change. Kevin White, director

NATURE'S ORCHESTRA, writer/producer
2015—A half-hour program for the KRCB PBS series *Natural Heroes* about the Arctic Soundscape Expedition led by the musician and nature sound recordist Bernie Krause

GREEN FIRE: ALDO LEOPOLD AND A LAND ETHIC FOR OUR TIME, writer
2011—An hour-long documentary about the life and legacy of Aldo Leopold. Winner, CINE Golden Eagle Award and Emmy Award for Best Historical Documentary. Steve Dunsky, director

MONTEREY BAY AQUARIUM VIDEOS, writer
2010—Three short videos for an exhibit on climate change titled *Hot Pink Flamingos: Stories of Hope in a Changing Sea*

CRUZ REYNOSO: SOWING THE SEEDS OF JUSTICE, writer
2009—An hour-long documentary about an inspiring jurist. Abby Ginzberg, director/producer

RIVER OF RENEWAL, writer/producer
2008—An hour-long documentary looking at the water and wildlife crisis in the Klamath Basin from the perspective of history. Winner, Best Documentary Feature, American Indian Film Festival. Carlos Bolado, director

LIVING WITH CHERNOBYL AND THE FUTURE OF NUCLEAR POWER, writer
2007—An hour-long documentary considering the outcome of the Chernobyl disaster twenty years afterwards and its implications for the debate about nuclear power in light of climate change. Red Door Productions

FIRE AND FOREST HEALTH, writer
2006—A DVD with a thirty-minute program and five special features about fire and forest ecology. Produced by Malcolm North

A LAND BETWEEN RIVERS, cowriter
2006—An hour-long history of Central California produced by Full Frame Productions for the Fresno County Historical Society. Winner, CINE Golden Eagle Award. Kevin White, director

THE BRIDGE SO FAR: A SUSPENSE STORY, writer
2005—An hour-long comedy news documentary about the San Francisco Bay Bridge replacement fiasco. Winner of two Emmy awards, including Best Documentary. David L. Brown, director

THE GREATEST GOOD, cowriter
2005—A two-hour documentary history of the US Forest Service produced to commemorate the centennial of the Forest Service by the USDA. Steve Dunsky, director

OIL ON ICE, writer
2004—An hour-long documentary video and website about the Arctic National Wildlife Refuge and the controversy over oil development there. Winner of Pare Lorentz Award. A Lobitos Creek Ranch Production

BRIDGING WORLD HISTORY, writer
2003—Four programs in a twenty-six-part series on world history produced by Oregon Public Broadcasting. Meighan Mahoney, series producer

PROMISES, researcher and consulting writer
2001—A feature-length documentary about children in and near Jerusalem—religious and secular Jews and Palestinians. An Academy Award nominee for Best Documentary. Emmys for Best Documentary and for Outstanding Background Analysis and Research. Promises Films

LIFE BEYOND EARTH, originator and coproducer
1999—Two-part series of hour-long science documentaries on the search for extraterrestrial life. Coproduced with KCTS 9, Seattle, for national PBS broadcast

RIVER OF THE WEST, writer
1996—A three-screen, twenty-minute film about the Columbia River, plus videos on logging and other kinds of work in Washington, a railroad story, and the Native Heritage, produced for the permanent exhibit of the Washington State History Museum. Lawrence Johnson Productions

DIFFERENT LENSES, writer
1996—Half-hour documentary about Edward S. Curtis and Asahel Curtis. Produced by KCTS 9, Seattle. Randy Brinson, director

FREEDOM ON MY MIND, consulting writer
1994—Feature-length documentary about the struggle for voting rights in Mississippi during the Freedom Summer of 1964. Academy Award nominee for Best Documentary. Clarity Productions

KUIPER: WINDOW ON THE UNIVERSE, writer
1994—Half-hour documentary about infrared astronomy from the Kuiper Airborne Observatory. Produced by NASA Ames

DOING JUSTICE: THE LIFE AND TRIALS OF ARTHUR KINOY, writer
1993—Fifty-minute biography of lawyer Arthur Kinoy, whose work included a last-minute Rosenberg defense and a successful challenge to the House Un-American Activities Committee. Abby Ginzberg, director/producer

BOUND BY THE WIND, writer
1993—Feature-length documentary about the history of nuclear testing and the international campaign for a Comprehensive Test Ban Treaty. David L. Brown, director

WONDERS OF NATURE, writer
1992—Hour-long film about the Grand Canyon, the Serengeti, the Sahara Desert, Iguazú Falls, the Amazon, Uluru, and the Himalayas. Winner of Emmys for Best Documentary and for Outstanding Cinematography. International Video Network and Reader's Digest

HEALTHY AGING, assistant producer/writer
1991—Hour-long documentary for PBS broadcast and videocassette distribution. KCET-TV. Michael Wiese, executive producer

BERKELEY IN THE SIXTIES, cowriter
1990—Feature-length documentary film about a generation's attempt to change the world. Academy Award nominee for Best Documentary. Mark Kitchell, director.

PLACES FOR THE SOUL, associate director/writer
1990—Half-hour documentary film about the architecture of Christopher Alexander. Ruth Landy, director/producer

THE POWER OF CHOICE, writer
1988—Eleven half-hour television programs about issues concerning teenagers. Hosted by Michael Pritchard. Broadcast nationally on PBS, cassette distribution to high schools. Elkind and Sweet Communications

LAS MADRES: THE MOTHERS OF THE PLAZA, consulting writer
1986—Hour-long documentary about the struggle of Argentinian mothers to recover their disappeared children. Academy Award nominee for Best Documentary. Muñoz Productions

 NOTES AND SOURCES

Stories Make the World

The storyteller Laura Simms once asked a fourth-grade class, "What would the world be like if there were no stories?" Immediately, a girl raised her hand. "If there were no stories," she said, "there would be no world. Stories make the world."

Simms tells that story in an audio documentary made by actor and playwright Corey Fisher and multimedia producer Claire Schoen. It gave them the title for the second show in a series called *Illuminations*, three hour-long documentaries based on plays created by A Traveling Jewish Theatre. They can be heard on http://claireschoenmedia.com/audio-programs/illuminations-jewish-culture-in-the-light-of-the-world-series-2007.

When I realized that *Stories Make the World* would be the right title for this book, I asked Corey and Claire for permission to use it.

Introduction

1. On the domestication of fire by hominids, see Yuval Noah Harari, *Sapiens* (New York: Harper Collins, 2015), pp. 12–13.
2. Antonio Damasio, *Self Comes to Mind* (New York: Random House, 2010), pp. 308–11.
3. Hannah Arendt, "Truth and Politics," in *Between Past and Future* (New York: The Viking Press, 1961), pp. 261–62.
4. Atul Gawande, "No Risky Chances," in *The Best American Science and Nature Writing 2015*, edited by Rebecca Skloot (New York: Houghton Mifflin Harcourt, 2015).
5. Ian McEwen, *Enduring Love* (New York: Anchor Books, 1997), p. 20.
6. For links to documentaries I have worked on that I discuss in these pages and for the scripts of plays I have written on related subjects, see www.stephenmost.com.

Part One: Storytellers

Pedro Azabache

1. I first learned about Pedro Azabache in John Gillin's *Moche: Peruvian Coastal Community* (London: Greenwood Press, 1947). A Cornell University summer field studies grant gave me the opportunity to meet him.
2. James Gleick, *The Information* (New York: Random House, 2011), pp. 416–17.
3. John Markoff, *Machines of Loving Grace* (New York: Harper Collins, 2015), p. 181.

Eduardo Calderon

1. Hannah Arendt, *The Human Condition* (Chicago: University of Chicago Press, 1958), p. 50.
2. Douglas Sharon, *Wizard of the Four Winds*, (New York: The Free Press, 1978), pp. 4–16.
3. In serving the priests by protecting their flock from sorcery, "white magic" *brujos* may have brought the *mesa* inside the church. That would account for the use of the Spanish word *mesa*, or table, as its name. The placing on a table of a symbolic microcosm that preserves the beliefs of "strangers in a strange land"—whether exiles in a diaspora or subjects of conquest by a foreign people who have transformed one's land—brings to mind the Jewish seder, the annual dinner party around a table laden with symbolic objects. On this occasion, stories that carry historical memories and express religious faith are retold.
4. In North America during the 1960s and '70s, shamanism became sensationalized as a magical adventure in the novels of Carlos Castaneda. He spun tales of mystical adventures with Don Juan, a Yaqui shaman in Mexico. Castaneda, who, like Douglas Sharon, got a PhD in anthropology at UCLA, was a Peruvian from Cajamarca, a town in the northern Andes that is a seedbed of *curanderismo*. Instead of revealing the presence of shamanism in the contemporary world as Sharon's film *Eduardo the Healer* does, the novelist transformed his knowledge of traditional healing ceremonies into a fantasy for the credulous. Influencing American youth in an era of alienation when many sought "a separate reality," to use one of Castaneda's titles, the Don Juan books succeeded through a kind of magic—the sorcery of a trickster.
5. Richard Meran Barsam, *Nonfiction Film: A Critical History* (New York: Dutton, 1973). pp. 128–29.
6. Robert Flaherty quoted in *Film Makers on Film Making,* edited by Harry M. Geduld (Bloomington: Indiana University Press, 1971), p. 57.
7. Roger Ebert's review of *Nanook of the North*, 25 September 2005, accessed December, 2016, URL: http://www.rogerebert.com/reviews/great-movie-nanook-of-the-north-1922.

Erik H. Erikson

1. In comparing his work as an analyst with shamanic storytelling, Erikson gave me an example: the story a Mexican healer tells women who have difficulties in labor. He guides them through a fantasy in which tiny creatures wearing pointed hats fight it out within the birth canal. Having a narrative puts one's pains into perspective, reducing anxiety. In this case, the shaman's story helps the patient relax and *dar luz*, the wonderful Spanish term for giving birth.
2. Erik H. Erikson, "Fishermen along a Salmon River," in *Childhood and Society* (New York: W. W. Norton, 1950), pp. 171–173.
3. Erikson published a fuller account of Fanny Flounder's psychotherapy in "Observations on the Yurok: Childhood and World Image," in *A Way of Looking at Things* (New York: W. W. Norton, 1987).
4. For an excellent biography of Erikson that looks at his life in its historical context, see Lawrence J. Friedman, *Identity's Architect* (Cambridge: Harvard University Press, 1999).
5. The quotes about the beginning of Erikson's career as a psychoanalyst come from a video interview he gave in his eighties to Harriet Harvey, who intended to make a documentary about his life and work. Having the same goal, director Danny Alpert and I saw her footage, and after Harvey's death, we negotiated rights to use those videos with her son, filmmaker Alex Gibney. Alpert and I were unable to get sufficient funding to make a full-length documentary; however, we did create a ten-minute version, *Identity Crisis*. It can be streamed on Vimeo: https://vimeo.com/kindlinggroup/erikson-trailer.
6. Friedman, *Identity's Architect*, p. 147.
7. Erikson, *Childhood and Society*, p. 38.
8. "Wholeness and Totality" is quoted in Friedman, *Identity's Architect*, p. 252.
9. Erik H. Erikson, *Dimensions of a New Identity* (New York: W. W. Norton, 1974), p. 27.
10. Erik H. Erikson, *Young Man Luther* (New York: W. W. Norton, 1958), p. 110.
11. Erik H. Erikson, *Gandhi's Truth* (New York: W. W. Norton, 1969), p. 431. Storytelling that turns fictions into unquestionable facts plays a part in the creation of a pseudo-species. "In the name of his pseudo-species," wrote Erikson, "man could endow himself and his universe with tools and weapons, roles and rules, with legends, myths, and rituals, which would bind his group together and give to its existence such super-individual significance as inspires loyalty, heroism, and poetry."
12. Stephen Most and Lynn Grasberg, coeditors, *The Broken Circle* (Palo Alto: Consulting Psychologists Press, 1989), pp. 52, 58. The Erikson chapter, "The Human Identity Crisis," was edited from a series of weekly interviews I conducted with Erikson during the mid-1980s, when he and Joan were living in the San Francisco Bay Area.
13. Erikson, *Gandhi's Truth*, p. 413.
14. Marshall Berman, "Erik Erikson, the Man Who Invented Himself," *New York Times*, 30 March 1975.
15. Erikson, *Young Man Luther*, pp. 111–12.

16. Erikson, *Childhood and Society,* pp. 34–41.
17. Erikson, *Gandhi's Truth,* p. 245.

Ginetta Sagan

1. I interviewed Ginetta Sagan for a documentary about her life that was never completed. She is the only source I have for the stories she told about her life. Documentation of her human rights campaigns is archived at Stanford University's Hoover Institution on War, Revolution, and Peace.
2. Vaclav Havel, *The Power of the Powerless* (Palach Press, 1985), p. 38.
3. Hannah Arendt, *The Human Condition* (Chicago: University of Chicago Press, 1958), p. 173.

Hannah Arendt

1. "The quest for meaning" is a phrase that recurs in Arendt's posthumously published *Thinking,* volume 1 of *The Life of the Mind* (Harcourt, Brace, Jovanovich, 1977). This quote appears on page 78.
2. Hannah Arendt, "What Remains?" in *Essays in Understanding* (Harcourt, Brace & Co., 1994), p. 3.
3. For an excellent study of Arendt as a storyteller, see Lisa Jane Disch, *Hannah Arendt and the Limits of Philosophy,* (Ithaca: Cornell University Press, 1994).
4. Hannah Arendt and Karl Jaspers, *Correspondence 1926–1969* (Harcourt, Brace, Jovanovich, 1992), p. 31.
5. Ibid., pp. 409–10.
6. Ibid. pp. 414–18.
7. Arendt refers to this encounter with the German journalist twice in correspondence that is published in English: in letters to her husband, Heinrich Blücher in *Within Four Walls* (Harcourt, Brace, 1996), p. 355, and to Karl Jaspers in *Correspondence,* p. 435. The account I use, quoting from memory, she gave at a class on the Nuremberg Trials in the course that she co-taught with Gerhard Casper, then a professor of law at the University of Chicago, for law students and graduate students in the Committee on Social Thought.
8. *Correspondence,* p. 417.
9. Hannah Arendt, *Eichmann in Jerusalem,* pp. 115, 117.
10. Ibid., pp. 49–50.
11. Hannah Arendt, "On Violence," in *Crises of the Republic* (New York: Harcourt, Brace, Jovanovich, 1969), p. 137.
12. *Correspondence,* p. 532.
13. Elizabeth Young-Bruehl, *For Love of the World* (Yale University Press, 1982), pp. 347–49.
14. Arendt, *Within Four Walls,* p. 387.
15. *Correspondence,* p. 511.
16. Hannah Arendt, *The Jewish Writings,* edited by Jerome Kohn and Ron H. Feldman (Schocken, 2007), p. 283.

17. Ibid., p. 303.
18. Norman Podhoretz, "Hannah Arendt on Eichmann: The Perversity of Brilliance," *Commentary*, 1 September 1963.
19. Hannah Arendt and Mary McCarthy, *Between Friends* (Harcourt, Brace, 1995), p. 168. In a *New York Times* "Bookends" essay, "Fifty Years Later, Why does Eichmann in Jerusalem Remain Contentious?", Adam Kirsch emphasizes the feelings of pride and shame that underlie the tone of *Eichmann and Jerusalem*. "A display of pride was for her a moral imperative, a way of showing her utter contempt for Nazism. . . . The necessary converse of pride, however, is shame, and whenever Arendt judges Jews to have acted unworthily, she expresses an acute sense of shame." 1 December 2013.
20. Hannah Arendt, "Truth and Politics," in *Between Past and Future* (Viking Press, 1968), pp. 227, 262.
21. Arendt, *Men in Dark Times*, p. 21.
22. Arendt, *Essays in Understanding*, p. 323.
23. Arendt, *The Human Condition*, p. 171.
24. Ibid., p. 188.
25. Arendt, *Men in Dark Times*, p. 24, 30.
26. Jonas's eulogy is unpublished.
27. For an account of Arendt and her friends in relation to *Eichmann in Jerusalem*, see Young-Bruehl, *For Love of the World*, pp. 351–53.
28. Bettina Stangneth, *Eichmann Before Jerusalem* (Knopf, 2014).
29. Mark Lilla, "Arendt & Eichmann: The New Truth," *New York Review of Books* (21 November 2013), p. 35.
30. The nutshell statement is from Hannah Arendt's "Action and 'The Pursuit of Happiness'" in the Library of Congress Hannah Arendt Papers, lecture, American Political Science Association, New York, NY, 1960, accessed December 2016, URL: https://memory.loc.gov/cgi-bin/ampage?collId=mharendt&fileName=05/051010/051010page.db&recNum=0:

> I have always believed that, no matter how abstract our theories may sound or how consistent our arguments appear, there are incidents and stories behind them which, at least for ourselves, contain as in a nutshell the full meaning of whatever we have to say. Thought itself—to the extent it is more than a technical, logical operation which electronic machines may be better equipped to perform than the human brain—arises out of the actuality of incident, and incidents of living experience must remain its guideposts by which it takes its bearing if it is not to lose itself.

31. Hannah Arendt, "Heidegger at Eighty," *New York Review of Books* (21 October, 1971).
32. Alexis de Tocqueville quoted in *Between Past and Future*, p. 7.
33. Martin Heidegger, *Being and Time* (Harper and Row, 1962), p. 165.
34. Günter Gauss, interview. The text is published in *Hannah Arendt: The Last Interview and Other Conversations* (Brooklyn: Melville House, 2013), pp. 3–38. A characteristic of totalitarian rule, as described in Hannah Arendt's *The Origins of Totalitarianism* (New York: Meridian Books, 1958), page 362, is its reliance on fictions. These thrive in the absence of alternative accounts and have an advantage over nonfiction in not being limited by experience and in being more logical and consistent than stories based on reality.

35. Arendt, *Men in Dark Times*, p. 8.
36. Alexander Klein, editor, *Dissent, Power, and Confrontation*, Theatre for Ideas/ Discussions 1, (New York: McGraw Hill, 1971), pp. 98–102.
37. Hannah Arendt, "Lying in Politics," in *Crises of the Republic*, p. 17–18.
38. Roger Berkowitz, "Introduction," in *Thinking in Dark Times*, edited by Roger Berkowitz, Jeffrey Katz, and Thomas Keenan (New York: Fordham University Press, 2010), p. 10.
39. Arendt, *Thinking*, p. 3.
40. Hannah Arendt, "Thinking and Moral Considerations in Responsibility and Judgment," in *Responsibility and Judgment*, edited by Jerome Kohn (New York: Schocken, 2003), pp. 188–89
41. Arendt, *Men in Dark Times*, p. 15.
42. Ibid., p. 105.
43. A statement regarding the importance of storytelling for Hannah Arendt concludes the fourteenth chapter of *Eichmann in Jerusalem*. Earlier, she told the story of Anton Schmidt, a sergeant in the German Army who helped members of the Jewish underground by making forged papers and military trucks available to them. He did so without asking for money in return. After supporting Jewish partisans for five months, Schmidt was arrested and executed. Arendt concluded that it would be of great benefit for the reputation of postwar Germany and "for her sadly confused internal condition, if there were more such stories to be told. For the lesson of such stories is simple and within everybody's grasp. Politically speaking, it is that under conditions of terror most people will comply but *some people will not*, just as the lesson of the countries to which the Final Solution was proposed is that "it could happen" in most places but *it did not happen everywhere*. Humanly speaking, no more is required, and no more can reasonably be asked, for this planet to remain a place fit for human habitation."

Part Two: Beginnings and Ends

Achilles' Shield

1. Yeats, "Sailing to Byzantium," in *The Collected Poems of W. B. Yeats* (New York: Macmillan, 1933), p. 191
2. Aeschylus, *The Persians*, translated by Anthony Podlecki (Prentice-Hall, 1970).
3. Homer, *The Iliad*, translated by Robert Fitzgerald (New York: Anchor Press/ Doubleday, 1974), book 7, p. 271.
4. Karl Jaspers, *The Origin and Goal of History* (New Haven: Yale University Press, 1953), p. 2.
5. Hannah Arendt, *Essays in Understanding, 1930–1954* (New York: Harcourt, Brace & Co., 1994), p. 20.
6. Hannah Arendt, "The Concept of History," in *Between Past and Future* (New York: Viking Press, 1961), p. 51; Hannah Arendt, "Action and 'The Pursuit of Happiness.'" Lecture, American Political Science Association, New York, NY 1960 (Series: Speeches and Writings File, 1923–1975) in the Library of

Congress Hannah Arendt Papers, accessed December, 2016, URL: https://memory.loc.gov/cgi-bin/ampage?collId=mharendt&fileName=05/051010/051010page.db&recNum=0.

7. Homer, *The Odyssey*, translated by Robert Fagles (New York: Viking Press, 1996), book 8.

8. Homer, *The Iliad*, book 18.

9. Werner Jaeger, *Paideia* (New York: Oxford University Press, 1939), pp. 140–42, 160.

10. H. D. F. Kitto, *The Greeks*, (Baltimore: Penguin Books, 1951), p. 104.

11. Jaeger, *Paideia*, pp. 227–31.

12. Aeschylus, *Agamemnon*, translated by Richmond Lattimore, *Aeschylus I*, (Chicago: University of Chicago Press, 1953), p. 44, , lines 160–63.

13. See Hannah Arendt on character and action in *The Human Condition*, Chapter 5, "Action," (Chicago: University of Chicago Press, 1958).

14. Susanne K. Langer, *Feeling and Form* (New York: Scribner's, 1953), p. 307.

15. Walter Benjamin, *Illuminations* (New York: Harcourt, Brace, 1968), p. 90.

16. Aeschylus, *The Oresteia*, translated by David Grene & Wendy Doniger O'Flaherty (Chicago: University of Chicago Press, 1989), p. 42.

17. I. F. Stone, "Holy War," *New York Review of Books* (3 August 1967).

18. Thucydides, *The Peloponnesian War*, translated by Rex Warner (Baltimore: Penguin Books, 1954), p. 24.

19. Walter Benjamin, quoted in Marie Luise Knott, *Unlearning with Hannah Arendt* (New York: Other Press, 2011), p. xi.

20. Tom Stoppard, "Shipwreck," in *The Coast of Utopia* (New York: Grove Press, 2002), p. 179.

21. Hannah Arendt, "The Concept of History," p. 51.

22. Robert Fulford, *The Triumph of Narrative* (New York: Broadway Books, 1999), p. 137.

23. Jean Paul Sartre quoted in Ricky D'Ambrose "A Theater without Qualities," *The Nation* (20 October 2014), p. 28.

24. Robert McKee, *Story* (London: Methuen, 1998), p. 49.

25. Lisa Randall, "Seeing Dark Matter as the Key to the Universe—and Human Empathy," *Boston Globe*, 26 October 2015, accessed December, 2016, URL: https://www.bostonglobe.com/opinion/2015/10/25/seeing-dark-matter-key-universe-and-human-empathy/NXNMBXAa7WEWejN63fFCNL/story.html.

26. Michael Moore, "13 Rules for Making Documentary Films," *Huffington Post*, 17 September 2014, accessed December, 2016, URL: http://www.huffingtonpost.com/michael-moore/13-rules-for-making-docum_b_5834954.html.

Fire in the Cave

1. Judith Thurman, "Letter from Southern France," *New Yorker* (23 June 2008).

2. Martin Scorsese, "The Persisting Vision: Reading the Language of Cinema," *New York Review of Books* (15 August 2013).

3. E. O. Wilson, *The Social Conquest of Earth* (W. W. Norton & Company, 2012), p. 287.

4. Ludwig Wittgenstein, *Philosophical Investigations*, #109 (New York: Macmillan, 1953), p. 47.

5. B. J. Bullert, *Public Television: Politics and the Battle over Documentary Film* (Rutgers University Press, 1997), p. 6.

6. David L. Brown, "Going Nuclear," *Release Print*, Film Arts Foundation, Summer 1992.

7. I wrote *Loon's Rage* with playwright Joan Holden and director Jael Weisman. It toured West Coast cities in 1977. After leaving Dell'Arte, I wrote another physical comedy about nuclear technology using the same California Indian animal characters: *Raven's Seed*.

8. In an email to me, Chris Beaver described the process of developing a three-act structure for *Dark Circle*. It required "a great deal of struggle. We worked with several consultants. A key moment was Ruth Landy's bringing Peter Adair onboard as a consultant. We essentially closed down the editing for a period of about a week while Peter gave us his seminar on the three-act structure. And also at a certain point Judy worked on her own for writing and structure with Susan Griffin, whose book *Woman and Nature: The Roaring Inside Her* was a major influence on our thinking. For me, the key point here and perhaps for others is that the three-act structure did not give up its secrets easily. . . . In retrospect we all look at our films and think, why didn't we just do it that way in the first place. Trial and error. Trial and error. And time. That's what our process took."

9. Christof Koch, *Consciousness* (MIT Press, 2012), p. 55.

10. B. J. Bullert's *Public Television: Politics and the Battle over Documentary Film* (1997) is my source for this account of the conflicted response to *Dark Circle* by public television.

11. Hannah Arendt in *Hannah Arendt's Lectures on Kant*, edited by Ronald Biener (University of Chicago, 1983), p. 43.

12. *Dark Circle* is available for educational distribution from The Video Project: http://www.videoproject.com/Dark-Circle.html. The consumer DVD can be ordered from Amazon.

13. Karl Kraus, *Beim Wort Genommen* (Munich: Koesel Verlag, 1955), p. 111.

Theater of History

1. *Different Lenses*, produced by KCTS Seattle in 1996.

2. Henry David Thoreau, *A Week on the Concord and Merrimack Rivers*, Google ebook, p. 344.

3. Aldo Leopold, *A Sand County Almanac* (Oxford University Press, 1948), pp. 224–25.

4. The transcript of my interview with Vi Hilbert is provided here with the permission of the Washington State Historical Society.

5. The Washington State History Museum was conceived as a theater of history. My book *In the Presence of the Past*, published by the Washington State Historical Society in 1996, describes some of the exhibits and their representation of history in detail.

6. E. O. Wilson, *The Future of Life* (New York: Knopf, 2002), p. 40.

7. Arendt said "the inalienable right to go visiting" in conversation. She was referring to Kant's concept of representative thinking as well as to the literal meaning of traveling to encounter others.

8. David Nicandri, the president of the Washington State Historical Society who oversaw the design and construction of the Washington State History Museum in Tacoma, commissioned me to write a play based on the dialogue between Leon and Mac in the Hooverville shack diorama. The original production of *A Free Country* by Seattle's Group Theatre occurred in the auditorium of the new museum as part of its inaugural celebration.

9. Unit 3, "Human Migrations" in *Bridging World History*, produced by Oregon Public Broadcasting for the Annenberg Foundation. I scripted four of the twenty-six programs, including that one.

Part Three: Natural World

On The Interstellarnet

1. Although Homer's cosmology is unknown, Achilles' shield, which portrays a cosmos encircled by the river Ocean, offers intriguing clues. That cosmos takes a circular form, an idea later expressed by the orbs and orbits of Ptolemy's universe. At the hub of the shield's concentric circles are "all the stars": "Pleiades, Hyades, Orion in his might, the Great Bear too. . ." Instead of the notion that the universe is out there, far away from the Earth, the imagery on Achilles' shield suggests that the stars are central to everything on Earth; the universe is within us all.

    Homer's placement of the stars at the hub of a human cosmos corresponds not only to the modern discovery that the heavy elements that form planets and living bodies are created within stars and exploded by supernovae into interstellar space. According to the Big Bang model of cosmology, the universe exploded from an infinitesimally small point that has expanded into everything, carrying galaxies, stars, planets and ourselves along for the ride. As this is a four-dimensional universe according to Einstein's theory of relativity, the expansion of time is inseparable from the inflation of space. Experimental cosmologist Richard A. Muller maintains in *NOW, The Physics of Time* (New York: W. W. Norton, 2016) that in sensing time as an ongoing now, our minds are experiencing the growth of the universe.

2. Vi Hilbert's story about the constellation's origin is told by a fisherman tending his net in a longhouse diorama in the permanent exhibit of the Washington State Historical Society. In the form of a monochromatic sculpture, the fisherman tells how the linguistically diverse peoples of Puget Sound created a common world. As she chose this tale for the diorama during our interview, Hilbert said there are stories a storyteller feels responsible for keeping alive. Here is her story:

    > On a winter night, when you look up at the sky, you can see three fishermen, with a fish below them, hanging from their canoe. Do you know how it was they got up into the sky?

When the Changer created everything in the world, he started in the East and worked toward the West. As he created each group of people, he gave each of them a language. But when he reached Puget Sound country, he still had a great number of languages left. So he scattered them all around. That is the reason why the people of the Sound speak so many different languages.

The people weren't satisfied with the way Changer had made the world. But they did not know what to do about it. They found that the sky was too low. The taller people would bump their heads on the sky. Wise leaders of the tribes agreed that the people could shove the sky higher if they all pushed together at the same time. But how could they do that if they did not speak the same language?

Finally, one of the wise men thought of the word *yeháw*, which means "to proceed." Soon the people spread the word. They agreed that *yeháw* was the signal to push the sky up.

Everybody made tall poles and braced them against the sky. When the word was given—*yeháw!*—all lifted as hard as they could. The sky went up, but not enough. So they lifted hard again and raised the sky a little higher. It took four pushes to raise the sky to its present position.

When the people did that, those three fishermen were canoeing where the water meets the sky, and they got pushed up, unable to come home ever again. There are four elk up there too, with three hunters walking on the trail after them. After chasing the elk for hours, the hunters were where the earth and the sky meet when suddenly the sky was lifted, taking them up too.

Everyone knows how that happened to them. And although we don't all speak the same language, everyone is happy that we were able to use that wonderful word *yeháw* to accomplish something together.

3. E. O. Wilson, *The Social Conquest of Earth* (New York: W. W. Norton & Company, 2012), p. 275.

4. Ralph Waldo Emerson, "Nature," in *The Essential Writings of Ralph Waldo Emerson*, edited by Brooks Atkinson (New York: Modern Library, 2000), p. 5.

5. I interviewed Joel Primack on 16 November 2008 for *Master of Light*, a documentary by Steve Michelson about his ancestor, the physicist and science educator Albert Michelson.

6. Nancy Abrams quoted in interview with Elizabeth Debold, *What is Enlightenment?* 40 (May–July 2008), p. 69. Joel Primack and Nancy Abrams wrote about the cosmic centrality of human experience in their book *The View From the Center of the Universe*, (New York: Riverhead Books, 2006).

7. Carl Sagan, *Cosmos: A Personal Voyage*, a thirteen-part series produced for PBS by KCET, 1980.

8. *Kuiper: Window On the Universe* is a half-hour documentary about infrared astronomy from the Kuiper Airborne Observatory.

9. After I interviewed her, Diane Wooden gave me a NASA photo of the Orion Nebula, a vast cloud of interstellar dust pierced by the light of nascent stars. It hangs in my study. This picture, taken through the Hubble Space Telescope, shows that my sense of beauty corresponds to the beauty of the universe. The idea that nature's deep design embodies beauty is the subject of *A Beautiful Question* (New York: Penguin, 2015) by Nobel Prize-winning physicist Frank Wilczek. Infrared imaging by the Hubble's successor, the James Webb Space Telescope, will reveal the birth of solar systems and a multitude of exoplanets within Orion and other stellar nurseries.

10. Frank Drake and Dava Sobel, *Is Anyone Out There?* (New York: Delacorte Press, 1992).
11. Yuval Noah Harari, *Sapiens* (New York: Harper Collins, 2015), pp. 32–36.
12. Erik H. Erikson, quoted in *The Broken Circle,* Stephen Most and Lynn Grasberg, coeditors, (Palo Alto: Consulting Psychologists Press, 1989), p. 53.
13. Carl Sagan was denied admission to the National Academy of Sciences, although he richly deserved that honor.
14. Timothy Ferris, *Seeing in the Dark* (New York: Simon & Shuster, 2002), p. 158.
15. Timothy Ferris quoted in Keay Davidson, *Carl Sagan, A Life* (New York: Wiley & Sons, 1999), p. 305.
16. Baruch Spinoza, "On the Improvement of the Understanding," in *Spinoza, Selections,* edited by John Wild (New York: Charles Scribner's Sons, 1930), p. 5.
17. Ralph Waldo Emerson, "The Poet," in *The Essential Writings of Ralph Waldo Emerson,* (New York: Random House, 2000), p. 293.
18. Christof Koch, *Consciousness* (Cambridge: MIT Press, 2012), p. 132.
19. Wilson, *The Social Conquest of Earth,* pp. 296–97.

The View from the Sierra Madre

1. Gillian Anderson, "A Fierce Green Fire: An Environmental Documentary So Honest You'll Want to Kill Yourself," *Stranger,* 3 April 2013. Although this series, directed and produced by Mark Kitchell, has a title derived from the writings of Aldo Leopold, it is not about Leopold and has nothing to do with *Green Fire,* the film that is the subject of this chapter. *Green Fire: Aldo Leopold and a Land Ethic for Our Time* premiered before Kitchell produced his series.
2. *The Greatest Good* is the US Forest Service Centennial Film. It can be ordered online: http://www.fs.fed.us/greatestgood/.
3. Aldo Leopold, *A Sand County Almanac* (Oxford: Oxford University Press, 1949), p. 110.
4. Curt Meine and Richard L. Knight, eds., *The Essential Aldo Leopold* (Madison: University of Wisconsin Press, 1999), p. 305.
5. Aldo Leopold, "The Land Ethic," in *A Sand County Almanac,* pp. 224–25.
6. Courtney White, "Living Leopold: the Land Ethic and a New Agrarianism," The Quivira Coalition's 8th Annual Conference (program), 4–6 November 2009, p. 3. URL accessed December, 2016: http://quiviracoalition.org/images/category/457-09%2520Conf%2520Program%2520web.pdf.
7. Aldo Leopold, "Thinking Like a Mountain," in *A Sand County Almanac,* p. 130.
8. Curt Meine, *Aldo Leopold, His Life and Work* (Madison: University of Wisconsin Press, 1988), p. 150.
9. Meine and Knight, eds., *The Essential Aldo Leopold,* p. 38.
10. Susan Flader, *Thinking Like a Mountain* (Madison: University of Wisconsin Press, 1974), p. 81.
11. Aldo Leopold, "Some Fundamentals of Conservation in the Southwest, 1923" quoted in Meine, *Aldo Leopold, His Life and Work,* pp. 213–14.
12. Leopold, "The Land Ethic," p. 178.

13. Aldo Leopold, "The Last Stand," in *The River of the Mother of God* (Madison: University of Wisconsin Press, 1991), p. 293.
14. Meine and Knight, eds., *The Essential Aldo Leopold*, p. 314.
15. Ibid., p. 148.
16. Leopold, "The Land Ethic," pp. 203–4.
17. *Green Fire: Aldo Leopold and a Land Ethic for Our Time* can be ordered from the Aldo Leopold Foundation: http://www.aldoleopold.org/greenfire/.

Upstream, Downstream

1. Shortly after the Salmon War, Lynn Adler, Jim Mayer, and other members of an independent film company called Ideas in Motion made a documentary about that crisis on the Klamath River. Completed in 1981, *Salmon on the Run* became an invaluable source of archival footage for *River of Renewal*, which went into production two decades later.
2. Aldo Leopold, "The Land Ethic," in *A Sand County Almanac* (Oxford University Press), p. 205.
3. Albert L. Kroeber and E. W. Gifford, *World Renewal: A Cult System of Native Northwest California*, vol. 13, *Anthropological Records* (Berkeley: University of California Press, 1949).
4. I write about the "War of Extermination" in *River of Renewal, Myth and History in the Klamath Basin* (Portland: Oregon Historical Society Press; Seattle: University of Washington Press, 2006), pp. 197–201.
5. My play *Medicine Show* draws from documentary sources about the Modoc War, including negotiation records, trial transcripts, and memoirs, many of which were written to a large extent in dialogue form. I also conducted a series of interviews with Leatha Chiloquin, a Modoc who learned through her family an oral history of the war. Regrettably, I did not record those interviews. My purpose was to gain insights for the play rather than to create a documentary resource that could serve historians, tribal members, and others.

   A research trip with the director and actors to the California lava beds where the war occurred and to Chiloquin, Oregon, where Leatha and her husband Edison Chiloquin lived, became the occasion for an historic event in twentieth-century upper basin history; for it was then that Edison, the grandson of Chief Chiloquin, held a sacred fire ceremony prior to reinhabiting his grandfather's village site. In doing so, Chiloquin gained national attention for his refusal to accept termination money and his determination to restore tribal lands. My news stories about his initiative attracted the support of American Indians who built and maintained with him a traditional village on the Sprague River. The sacred fire did not bring back Chief Chiloquin's world, but it ignited a process that led to the reestablishment of tribal government in the upper basin.

   The Klamath Tribes (including the Modocs and the Yahooskin) played an important part in the twenty-first-century conflict over the fish and water of the Klamath Basin. Their fishery research contributed to the biological opinions that led to the curtailment of irrigation water for Klamath Project farmers, and their senior water rights motivated farmers and ranchers to negotiate the Upper Basin Comprehensive Agreement with them in order to receive water that flows through tribal lands.

6. Carbon dating of redwood from the Indian house that was Geneva Mattz's ancestral home showed it to be at least six hundred years old.

7. My play *Watershed* draws from my memories of Geneva Mattz and her family during the Salmon War and afterwards and from the Mattz family oral history interviews by Helene Oppenheimer, which are available at the Bancroft Library, University of California, Berkeley. URL accessed December, 2016: http://www.oac.cdlib.org/search?style=oac4;titlesAZ=m;idT=UCb110145823.

8. Forrest J. Gerard, assistant secretary of Indian Affairs, issued this statement on 20 November 1978.

9. I describe the Klamath Basin stakeholders' workshops in Chapter Eighteen of *River of Renewal, Myth and History in the Klamath Basin.*

10. Jacques Leslie, "Rough Water," *Earth Island Journal,* Spring 2010. URL accessed December, 2016: http://www.earthisland.org/journal/index.php/eij/article/roughwater. The reconciliation process incorporated additional farmers and ranchers in the upper basin during the drought year of 2013 after Oregon recognized the senior water rights of the Klamath Tribes.

11. DVDs of *River of Renewal* can be ordered online from www.riverofrenewal.org and from The Video Project: http://www.videoproject.com/River-of-Renewal.html.

Part Four: Human World

Imagining Freedom

1. Hannah Arendt, "The Concept of History," in *Between Past and Future* (New York: Viking Press, 1961), p. 45.

2. Hannah Arendt, "Understanding and Politics," in *Essays in Understanding 1930–1954* (New York: Harcourt, Brace & Co., 1994), p. 323.

3. Hannah Arendt, *The Origins of Totalitarianism* (New York: Meridian Books, 1958), p. 362.

4. Hannah Arendt, "What is Freedom?" in *Between Past and Future,* p. 155.

5. Tom Stoppard, *The Coast of Utopia* (New York: Grove Press, 2002).

6. James Atlas, "Is This the End?" in *The New York Times,* 24 November 2012.

7. *Freedom on My Mind* is distributed by California Newsreel: http://newsreel.org/video/FREEDOM-ON-MY-MIND.

8. Connie Field was well aware of the historical context of the Mississippi Summer. Not until the larger history was portrayed in the fourteen-part series *Eyes on the Prize* did she decide to make *Freedom on My Mind.* Field went on to make her own epic history series, *Have You Heard from Johannesburg?* This seven-part documentary recounts the international movement to end apartheid.

9. Isaiah Berlin, "Two Concepts of Liberty," in *Four Essays on Liberty.* (Oxford: Oxford University Press, 2002).

10. *Berkeley in the Sixties* is distributed by California Newsreel: http://newsreel. org/video/BERKELEY-IN-THE-SIXTIES.
11. Susan Griffin, *Made from this Earth* (New York: Harper and Row, 1983), p. 3.

Land of Plenty

1. John McPhee, *Assembling California* (New York: Farrar, Straus and Giroux, 1993), p. 539.
2. Aldo Leopold, "Wherefore Wildlife Ecology?" (unpublished manuscript, 1947), p. 51.
3. Catherine M. Rehart, *The Heartland's Heritage* (Carlsbad: Heritage Media Corporation, 2000), pp. 60–61.
4. Kevin Starr, *Coast of Dreams* (New York: Vintage, 2006), pp. 496–98.
5. Cynthia J. Wright and Judy Cox-Finney, *Leemore* (Charleston: Arcadia Publishing, 2010), p. 41.
6. David Brooks, "A Nation of Mutts," *The New York Times*, 27 June 2013.

Fields of Centers

1. Christopher Alexander, *A Pattern Language* (New York: Oxford University Press, 1977).
2. Christopher Alexander, *Battle for the Life and Beauty of the Earth*, (Oxford: Oxford University Press, 2012), p. 58.
3. Christopher Alexander, *The Nature of Order*, vol. 1, *The Phenomenon of Life* (Berkeley: The Center for Environmental Structure, 2002), pp. 3–4.
4. Sarah Bakewell, *How to Live: Or A Life of Montaigne in One Question and Twenty Attempts at an Answer* (New York: Other Press, 2010), p. 77.
5. Isaiah Berlin, "The Pursuit of the Ideal," in *The Crooked Timber of Humanity* (New York: Knopf, 1991), pp. 5–11.
6. Hannah Arendt, "Truth and Politics," in *Between Past and Future* (New York: Viking Press, 1961), p. 242.
7. Christopher Alexander, *The Nature of Order*, vol. 4, *The Luminous Ground* (Berkeley: The Center for Environmental Structure, 2002), pp. 331–34.

Through the Wall

1. Hannah Arendt, *The Origins of Totalitarianism* (New York: Meridian Books, 1958), p. 157.
2. Elie Wiesel's acceptance speech is found at http://www.sfponline.org/ Uploads/66/ElieWieselspeech.pdf. URL accessed December, 2016.
3. Arendt, *The Origins of Totalitarianism*, pp. 235–36.
4. DVDs of *Promises* can be ordered via http://www.rocofilms.com/film. php?code=PROM. The children's reunion prior to the Academy Awards ceremony in 2002 is the subject of a special feature on the DVD.
5. Stream *In the Image* via https://www.kanopystreaming.com/product/ image-palestinian-women-capture-occupation.

6. For an interview with the filmmakers, see Michelle Chen, "Critical Exposure: Cameras in Hand, Palestinian Women Document Daily Abuses," *Truthout*, 7 December 2015. http://www.truth-out.org/news/item/33935-critical-exposure-cameras-in-hand-palestinian-women-document-daily-abuses. URL accessed December, 2016.

7. Rabbi Elitzur-Hershkowitz and Rabbi Yitzak Shapira, *Torat Hamelech* (The King's Torah), *The Book of Numbers* 33:52–56.

8. David Shulman, "Israel & Palestine: Breaking the Silence," *New York Review of Books* (27 January 2011).

9. *Occupation of the Territories: Israeli Soldier Testimonies 2000–2010* (Jerusalem: Breaking the Silence, 2010).

10. Akiva Eldar, "Israel Admits It Revoked Residency Rights of a Quarter Million Palestinians," *Haaretz* (12 June 2012). URL accessed December, 2016: www.haaretz.com/Israel-news/Israel-admits-it-revoked-residency-rights-of-a-quarter-million-palestinians-1.435778.

11. "Land Expropriation and Taking Control of the Land," B'Tselem.org, "Settlements," 1 January 2011. URL accessed December, 2016: www.btselem.org/settlements/land_takeover.

12. *The Law in These Parts* was produced by Ra'anan Alexandrowicz and Liran Atzmor. It had broadcasts on PBS's POV series in 2013.

13. For more on the movement to establish a Kingdom of Israel, demolish Al-Aqsa, and build the third temple on Temple Mount, see Ari Shavit, *My Promised Land* (New York: Spiegel and Grau, 2013), pp. 215–21.

Part Five: The Anthropocene

Baked Alaska

DVDs of *Oil On Ice* are available via www.oilonice.org.

1. Jiping Liu, Judith A. Curry, Yongjiu Dai, and Radley Horton, "Causes of the Northern High-Latitude Land Surface Winter Climate Change," *Geophysical Research Letters* 34 (18 July 2007).

2. Igor Krupnik and Dyanna Jolly, *The Earth is Faster Now, Indigenous Observations of Arctic Climate Change* (Fairbanks: Arctic Research Consortium of the United States, 2002).

3. Alexis de Tocqueville, *Democracy in America*, book 2, chapter 5. (New York: A. A. Knopf, 1945).

4. An examination of the role of lying in politics, one form of which is the discrediting of factual truth as if it were opinion, is found in Hannah Arendt's essay, "Truth and Politics," in *Between Past and Future* (New York: The Viking Press, 1961), pp. 227–64.

5. Rebecca Solnit, *The Faraway Nearby* (New York: Viking, 2013), pp. 154–59.

Sounds of a Changing Planet

1. Ralph Waldo Emerson, "Ode," in *The Essential Writings of Ralph Waldo Emerson* (New York: Modern Library, 2000), p. 694.
2. Henry David Thoreau, "Walking," *Atlantic Monthly* (May 1862).
3. Linnie Marsh Wolfe, *John of the Mountains: The Unpublished Journals of John Muir,* (Madison: University of Wisconsin Press, 1979), p. 99.
4. Michael Shellenberger and Ted Nordhaus's *Break Through: From the Death of Environmentalism to the Politics of Possibility* (Boston: Houghton Mifflin Company, 2007) makes the comparison between evangelical narratives and the death-of-nature trope of the environmental movement.
5. Rachel Carson, *Silent Spring* (Boston: Houghton Mifflin, 1962), pp. 1–3.
6. Aldo Leopold, *A Sand County Almanac* (Oxford: Oxford University Press, 1948), p. 149.
7. The Nature's Orchestra DVD and Study Guide are distributed by The Video Project: http://www.videoproject.com/Natures-Orchestra-Sounds-of-Our-Changing-Planet.html.
8. Bernie Krause, *Into a Wild Sanctuary* (Berkeley: Heyday Books, 1998), pp. 1–3.
9. Arctic Soundscape Expedition interview with Clara Jeffery, the editor of *Mother Jones*. She interviewed Krause in June 2006 inside a tent in the Arctic National Wildlife Refuge.
10. Bernie Krause, *The Great Animal Orchestra* (New York: Little, Brown & Company, 2012), pp. 84–85.
11. Several film festivals that screened *Nature's Orchestra* have held soundscape ecology nature walks followed by demonstrations of nature sound recordings on spectrograms. Prior to the Visions of the Wild festival, the Mare Island Technical Academy, a charter middle and high school, brought 130 students to conservation lands near Vallejo, California to record biophony and the geophony they encountered there. Drawing from this experience and from decades of teaching science at the Mare Island academy, Laurie Guest developed curricula to incorporate the science of sound, including soundscape ecology, into classroom instruction plans for grades 6 through 12.
13. Aldo Leopold, *A Sand County Almanac*, p. 149.

The Rim of the World

1. Medvedev is quoted in the Wikipedia entry "2010 Russian wildfires": https://en.wikipedia.org/wiki/2010_Russian_wildfires. URL accessed December, 2016.
2. Josh White is quoted in B. J. Hansen, *California's Rim Fire* (self-published, 2015), p. 71.
3. Stephen Pyne, *Between Two Fires* (Tucson: University of Arizona Press, 2015), p. 235.
4. Chad Hanson, "The Ecological Importance of California's Rim Fire," *Earth Island Journal* 28 (August 2013).

5. Mark E. Swanson, Jerry F. Franklin, Robert Beschta, Chris M. Crisafulli, Dominick A. DellaSala, Richard L. Hutto, David B. Lindenmeyer, and Frederick J. Swanson, "The Forgotten Stage of Forest Succession: Early Successional Ecosystems on Forest Sites," *Frontiers in Ecology and the Environment* 9, no. 2 (2 March 2010).

6. I dramatized the relationship between Muir and Pinchot in my play *Forces of Nature*. Both Muir and Pinchot were high-context advocates. Their contexts differed: revering the natural world, Muir created the first environmental movement. Valuing nature for human uses, Pinchot built a conservation agency within the federal government. The play's third character is Theodore Roosevelt, who deeply admired Muir while developing his administration's conservation policies with Pinchot.

   Forces of Nature represents the struggle between Muir and Pinchot over the fate of Hetch Hetchy Valley as a conflict of right against right. Although many environmentalists and conservationists are polarized politically—interpreting their differences in terms of low-context advocacy—historically, the antagonistic stances of Muir and Pinchot proved to be complementary. Without opposition from the passionate environmentalist, Pinchot could probably not have mustered enough political support to establish the national forest. Had the Forest Service not succeeded in managing millions of acres of public lands, most of the wilderness areas that realize Muir's preservationist vision would be in private hands today.

   Muir gave eloquent expression to a high-context worldview in writing, "When we try to pick out anything by itself, we find it hitched to everything else in the universe." John Muir, *My First Summer in the Sierra* (Boston: Houghton Mifflin, 1911), p. 110 of the Sierra Club Books 1988 edition.

7. Pyne, *Between Two Fires*, p. 221.

8. Malcolm North, Peter Stine, Kevin O'Hara, William Zielinski, and Scott Stephens, "An Ecosystem Management Strategy for Sierran Mixed-Conifer Forests," USDA Forest Service Pacific Southwest Station General Technical Report PSW-GTR-220, March 2009.

9. Malcolm North, S. L. Stephens, B. M. Collins, J. K. Agee, G. Applet, J. F. Franklin, and P. Z. Fulé, "Reform Forest Fire Management," *Science* 349, no. 6254 (18 September 2015).

10. The springboard for my thinking about megafires in the context of human history is the work of Stephen Pyne. "We are the keystone species for Earth's fire. We hold a species monopoly," he wrote in his essay "Green Fire Meets Red Fire" (forthcoming in a book Pyne is editing with Ben A. Minteer). The perception of human beings as a symbol-minded fire species draws also from Ernst Cassirer, *An Essay on Man* (New Haven: Yale University Press, 1944) and from Yuval Noah Harari, *Sapiens* (New York: Harper Collins, 2015).

Epilogue

1. Sandy Tolan, "The Voice and the Place," in *Reality Radio*, edited by John Biewen and Alexa Dilworth (Chapel Hill: University of North Carolina Press, 2010).
2. Hannah Arendt describes the world as being "common to all of us and distinguished from our privately owned place within it. . . . To live together in the world means essentially that a world of things is between those who have it in common, as a table is located between those who sit around it; the world, like every in-between, relates and separates men at the same time." *The Human Condition* (Chicago: University of Chicago Press, 1958), p. 52.

INDEX